*Responsive Practice for Dual Language Learners
in Early Childhood Education*

Responsive Practice for Dual Language Learners in Early Childhood Education

THEORY AND CASE STUDIES

JENNIFER J. CHEN, EDD

www.redleafpress.org
800-423-8309

Published by Redleaf Press
10 Yorkton Court
St. Paul, MN 55117
www.redleafpress.org

© 2025 by Jennifer J. Chen

All rights reserved. Unless otherwise noted on a specific page, no portion of this publication may be reproduced or transmitted in any form or by any means, electronic or mechanical, including photocopying, recording, or capturing on any information storage and retrieval system, without permission in writing from the publisher, except by a reviewer, who may quote brief passages in a critical article or review to be printed in a magazine or newspaper, or electronically transmitted on radio, television, or the internet.

First edition 2025
Cover design by Jesse Hughes
Cover illustration by Marharyta—adobe.stock.com
Interior design by Wendy Holdman
Typeset in Sirba and Acumin Pro
Printed in the United States of America
31 30 29 28 27 26 25 24   1 2 3 4 5 6 7 8

Library of Congress Cataloging-in-Publication Data
Names: Chen, Jennifer J., author.
Title: Responsive practice for dual language learners in early childhood education: theory and case studies / by Jennifer J. Chen.
Description: First edition. | St. Paul, MN : Redleaf Press, 2025. | Includes bibliographical references and index. | Summary: "This book provides educators theoretical background and practical advice as they welcome an increasing number of dual language learners into their programs, to support these children to learn and flourish. Author Jennifer Chen shares case studies from her fieldwork with diverse early childhood classrooms, demonstrating her Four Cornerstones of Responsive Practice framework while offering reflective questions to help educators implement it in their own contexts"—Provided by publisher.
Identifiers: LCCN 2024015287 (print) | LCCN 2024015288 (ebook) | ISBN 9781605548098 (paperback) | ISBN 9781605548104 (ebook)
Subjects: LCSH: Bilingualism in children—Philosophy. | Bilingualism in children—Case studies. | Language and languages—Study and teaching (Early childhood)—Philosophy. | Language and languages—Study and teaching (Early childhood)—Case studies.
Classification: LCC LC3723 .C56 2025 (print) | LCC LC3723 (ebook) | DDC 370.117/5—dc23/eng/20240501
LC record available at https://lccn.loc.gov/2024015287
LC ebook record available at https://lccn.loc.gov/2024015288

Printed on acid-free paper

To Jasmine, Alex, and Lizzy

Contents

Acknowledgments ix

PART I: THEORY

Chapter 1: Introduction: Teaching DLLs 3

Chapter 2: Reflective Practice 11

Chapter 3: Increasing Superdiversity 17

Chapter 4: Language Skills: Receptive, Expressive, BICS, and CALP 27

Chapter 5: The Four Cornerstones of Responsive Practice Framework 35

PART II: CASE STUDIES

Chapter 6: Providing Responsive Teacher Scaffolding 45

Chapter 7: Building Strong Teacher-Family and Teacher-Teacher Partnerships 67

Chapter 8: Supporting Learners with Special Needs 91

Chapter 9: Conclusion: Heart Work and Hard Work 109

References 113

Index 121

About the Author 131

Acknowledgments

As a Chinese-English bilingual, I find that learning about and teaching dual language learners (DLLs) is a topic of both personal and professional significance to me. Since publishing my previous book (*Connecting Right from the Start: Fostering Effective Communication with Dual Language Learners*, Gryphon House, 2016), I have been eager to pen another book on supporting the learning and development of DLLs. With this new book, my fresh proposal of the Four Cornerstones of Responsive Practice framework is born. This book also represents my newest approach to translating abstract theory into concrete practice by including the often-unsung reflective voices of early childhood educators who directly nurture the learning and development of culturally and linguistically diverse learners in the United States. However, I was only able to successfully bring to life these practical insights through the invaluable contributions from dedicated early childhood teachers who graciously lent their voices. Both the personal and professional support from others were also vital to this writing project. For that, they all deserve recognition here:

- With immense thanks to all twelve early childhood teacher contributors (Josephine Ahmadein, Vanessa Casella, Alexandra Diaz, Megan DiGuilio, Tiffany Enciso-Williams, Samantha Kaufman, Helen Papoutsakis, ChareMone' Perez, Fatima Rafhan, Lissette Ruiz, Imelda Stiles, and Erin Vaccaro) for entrusting me with their authentic voices.
- With gratitude to Kean University President Lamont O. Repollet for granting me sabbatical leave, during which I had the time to reflect on and delve into my new ideas, laying the very foundation for this book. I am also grateful to Kean provost and senior vice president for Academic Affairs, David S. Birdsell, and College of Education acting dean Sancha K. Gray, for their support of my scholarly endeavors.

Acknowledgments

- With appreciation to Christina Sbarro, my capable graduate research assistant (supported by Kean University), for proofreading this manuscript and adding some ideas to two case analyses.
- With gratitude to Melissa York, senior editor at Redleaf Press, whose encouraging and supportive feedback was invaluable in refining some of my ideas and the overall organization of this book. Special thanks also to Marcella Weiner for her constructive feedback as well as to Douglas Schmitz and the entire Redleaf Press team for their efforts in bringing this book to fruition. The thought-provoking queries from both Melissa and Marcella encouraged and challenged me to translate knowledge often confined to the ivory tower of academia into a responsive "language" that would resonate with educators.
- With fond memory of my beloved grandparents—who taught me many lessons in life by example.
- With profound gratitude to my parents for giving me life, nurturing my learning and development during my early years, and providing me with the opportunity to acquire English as a second language and experience diverse cultures in the United States up close during my teenage years. This latter experience has significantly shaped my understanding of language learning and deepened my appreciation for cultural diversity.
- With heartfelt gratitude to my immediate family. My husband, Eric Lin, is my enduring coteacher and colearner in our parenting journey. With infinite love to our very own dual language learners, Jasmine, Alexander, and Lizette, who are my greatest inspiration and "bestest" teachers in my continuous journey of learning to better educate children.
- I am forever grateful to God—my constant in a constantly changing world—for all the blessings.

Part I: Theory

CHAPTER 1

Introduction: Teaching DLLs

To learn a language is to have one more window from which to look at the world.

—Widely attributed as a Chinese proverb

Language is vital for it offers a critical lens for us to view and shape the world in which we live. Through language, we come to understand many things and concepts, including our surroundings, cultures, ideas, relationships, people, and even ourselves. From this perspective, language is an invaluable resource that we should acquire and savor. It also means that the more languages we know, the more lenses we can apply to view and understand the world. This makes a compelling case for fostering bilingualism/biculturalism or multilingualism/multiculturalism in ourselves (to the extent possible) and in the children we educate.

In particular, language is critical for all aspects of learning and development. We use it all the time for all kinds of functions, including accessing and processing knowledge, communicating with one another, problem solving, negotiating our viewpoints, and ultimately navigating the diverse world in which we live. In the same vein, language also plays a fundamental role in everyday social interactions and the educational success of children. In essence, language is power. However, to harness and wield the power of language effectively, we must first acquire it and then maintain our language proficiencies. For culturally and linguistically diverse learners who are trying to apply and maintain their home language, it is imperative that their teachers engage in developmentally, culturally, linguistically, and contextually responsive practice that respects and supports their home language development.

Within the population of culturally and linguistically diverse learners in early childhood education settings, many are considered dual language learners. The term *dual language learners* (DLLs) was coined by the Office of Head Start (2008) to refer to young children who are learning two or more languages concurrently or acquiring a second language (L2) while simultaneously mastering their first language (L1). While responsive practice benefits all children, DLLs have unique developmental, cultural, linguistic, and contextual needs that require specific types of teacher support.

Glimpses into the World of Teaching through the Eyes of the Teachers

Teaching young children, especially those from culturally and linguistically diverse backgrounds, is a particularly complex task. It is a highly demanding responsibility that requires a considerable amount of physical energy (e.g., stamina), mental energy (e.g., decision-making), and emotional energy (e.g., patience). In addition, there lies the intellectual aspect of the teaching profession that calls for teachers to be pedagogically effective—that is, that teachers should deliver curriculum content effectively to facilitate optimal student learning. Amid these physically, mentally, emotionally, and intellectually consuming activities, in their daily teaching work, teachers likely make numerous decisions in an array of situations (both expected and unexpected). There is no manual for successful decision-making. Nonetheless, teachers are often expected to exercise their professional judgment and apply their professional expertise when making decisions and solving problems in their teaching. For instance, the conscious decision to scaffold the learning and development of culturally and linguistically diverse learners is a common one among the early childhood educators featured in this book, as reflected in their case narratives.

I strongly believe that by reflecting intentionally on their practice, teachers can better navigate the often complex contours of teaching. Thus, the main contents of this book are constructed using a reflective practice approach to understanding and analyzing early childhood teachers' decision-making and actions in educating their DLLs. Through the teachers' narrated reflective practices, we are invited into their teaching world, viewing it through their eyes to glimpse into the realities of their everyday work: the joy, the struggle, the resolution, the opportunities, and the challenges—everything and anything in between that makes teaching a continuous journey of professional learning and growth. It is important to recognize that while these glimpses may highlight what stood out for these teachers, they do not depict the whole picture. Instead, they provide only snapshots of their vital work with culturally and linguistically diverse learners. Nonetheless, even within these snapshots, we bear witness to the power of teacher voices—a key feature of this book.

The Power of Teacher Voices

I was compelled to capture and amplify the often-unsung unique voices of early childhood educators in the field. To do so, I presented their reflective narratives recounting specific instances of working with culturally and linguistically diverse learners, especially DLLs and their families. By intentionally drawing on the authentic voices of early childhood educators, this book invites other educators to join the conversation. It also encourages them to dive into the reflective process to think about and rethink their own teaching practices. Furthermore, the reflective narratives captured in this book may resonate with other educators in ways that affirm, reaffirm, or even disaffirm their current practices in working with DLLs.

The approach of situating the case narratives within a reflective framework acknowledges that educators engage with and navigate the complex world of teaching from their unique viewpoints. These perspectives, in turn, serve as the foundation for the educators' own meaning making and interpretation of their individual teaching experiences. This book further emphasizes the importance of reflective practice for educators' professional growth by presenting authentic classroom examples where teachers reflect, make decisions, and take actions accordingly.

The Power of Reflective Practice

When the teachers' decision-making is galvanized by their reflection on their teaching and student learning, it can lead to reflective practice. To a certain extent, teachers are expected to seamlessly translate theory into a particular instructional practice. When there is a particular program, curriculum, or intervention that teachers are expected to implement, it is critical that teachers depart from the technical rationality of teaching (Dewey 1933; Schön 1983, 1987). Instead, they should think outside the box to extract or adjust whatever theoretical principles that might fit their specific classroom situations. That is, effective teachers do not just implement a program, curriculum, or intervention at its face value, they consider contextual factors, such as the unique learning needs of individual children and the diverse socioeconomic, cultural, and linguistic backgrounds of their families. By incorporating knowledge of these factors, teachers can better engage in reflective practice by adapting their teaching accordingly to meet these contextual circumstances. In doing so, the teachers can become intentional in reflective practice. For instance, the National Association for the Education of Young Children's (NAEYC's) (2020) developmentally appropriate practice calls for early childhood educators to apply intentionality in planning and delivering purposeful, joyful, achievable, engaging, and meaningful learning experiences for young children, including building partnerships with families. It is also imperative that these educators are intentional in instructional decision-making, assessment, and strategies to better scaffold the learning and development of children from culturally and linguistically diverse backgrounds (Chen 2016a). Taken together, effective early childhood educators are viewed as those who engage intentionally in developmentally appropriate practice by supporting the common development of the whole child in all domains, the diverse learning needs of individual children, as well as the social (e.g., family, community) and cultural (e.g., values, beliefs, language backgrounds) contexts in which learning and development occur for these children (NAEYC 2022).

While articulating a set of theoretical principles to guide practice, NAEYC (2022, 49) also urged early childhood educators, as lifelong learners, to "cultivate the habit of reflective and intentional practice in their daily work with young children and as members of the early childhood profession." Despite its critical importance, reflection is not necessarily a habitual practice for educators. While teachers are presented with opportunities to reflect, they may not always know how to do it or do it well. I hope that the case narratives offer needed glimpses and guidance into what reflective practice in action looks like. While reflective practices are evident through the case studies presented throughout the chapters in the second part of this book, they also demonstrate that there is no one-size-fits-all solution to all teaching situations. However, certain principles, such as the Four Cornerstones of Responsive Practice framework proposed here, can serve as essential guidance to these situations.

The Four Cornerstones of Responsive Practice Framework

This book centers on the application of what I term the *Four Cornerstones of Responsive Practice framework*, reflecting (1) developmental responsiveness, (2) cultural responsiveness, (3) linguistic responsiveness, and (4) contextual responsiveness. NAEYC (2020, 2022) subsumed these areas under the umbrella of *developmentally appropriate practice*. However, this umbrella term might steer some educators into viewing child development as a singular dimension. To make clear that developmentally appropriate practice is actually made up of specific, key elements, I delineate the four dimensions of responsive practice individually as representing Four Cornerstones. The use of the term *Four Cornerstones* is intentional and metaphorical to suggest that the four elements are grounded collectively as the essential foundation on which effective teaching is built. Furthermore, while these four dimensions hold their own individual significance, they are all interconnected to form a collective whole that revolves around the child at the center. That is, each area does not operate alone; instead, it is considered within the premise that the whole is greater than the sum of its parts. For instance, we cannot claim that we are engaging in developmentally responsive practice if we do not consider the cultural, linguistic, and contextual characteristics of the children whom we are educating. Similarly, we cannot declare that we are practicing cultural responsiveness if we disregard children's development at their own levels and paces. By understanding and incorporating these Four Cornerstones of Responsive Practice, we can better create an environment that supports and nurtures both the common and unique developmental, cultural, linguistic, and contextual strengths and needs of each young learner. Importantly, this model serves as an equitable, just, and inclusive lens to affirm, inform, and transform practices so they become centered on responsiveness. However, responsive practice does not occur in a vacuum: they are intricately linked to teacher reflection, and, by extension, to professional learning and growth, as discussed in the next chapter.

Book Organization and Content Coverage

This book is organized into two parts, spanning nine chapters: part 1 on theory, containing the introductory chapter and four other chapters, and part 2 on practices, including three chapters that feature case studies and the concluding chapter. Each chapter begins with a topic-inspired epigraph designed to provoke thought and reflection linked to the chapter content and ends with a conclusion accompanied by reflection questions to stimulate further discussion.

In part 1, the current chapter (chapter 1) affirms the imperative of supporting the learning and development of culturally and linguistically diverse learners, the power of teacher voices, and the importance of reflective practice. It also introduces the key feature of this book—the Four Cornerstones of Responsive Practice framework. Chapter 2 delves deeper into the concept of reflective practice, including discussing what it is, why it is important, and how it should be conducted. Chapter 3 highlights the phenomenon of superdiversity and its implications for educating DLLs. Chapter 4 describes four foundational yet essential language skills for children to acquire (receptive skills, expressive skills, basic interpersonal communication skills, and cognitive academic language proficiency). Chapter 5 delineates my proposed Four Cornerstones of Responsive Practice, which will be used as the framework for analyzing the case studies in part 2 of this book.

In part 2, the chapters are woven together to amplify the authentic voices of twelve early childhood educators in their narrated reflective case studies. Chapter 6 describes four case studies illustrating how teachers address the language needs of DLLs through proper scaffolding:

- Megan DiGuilio (a prekindergarten teacher) scaffolded the learning of English and social skills of a Spanish-speaking DLL.
- Fatima Rafhan (a preschool teacher) scaffolded a Ukrainian-English DLL's acquisition of language skills using a variety of strategies.
- Imelda Stiles (a kindergarten English-Spanish bilingual teacher) scaffolded her DLLs' learning of rhyming in Spanish and their transfer of this cognitive skill to English.
- ChareMone' Perez (a second-grade teacher of DLLs in a Spanish-English bilingual classroom) scaffolded her DLLs in learning to produce descriptive essays as part of academic writing in English.

Chapter 7 presents another set of four case studies featuring how teachers cultivate strong and positive teacher-family partnerships to enhance DLLs' educational experiences:

- Josephine Ahmadein (an infant/toddler Spanish-English bilingual educator) cultivated a connection with a child by first establishing a positive connection with his family.
- Alexandra Diaz (a preschool teacher) acquired some Portuguese to communicate with a Brazilian child and establish a positive partnership with this child's family.
- Samantha Kaufman (a prekindergarten teacher) facilitated a family's understanding of what an individualized education program/plan (IEP) means and entails.
- Helen Papoutsakis (a first-grade teacher) fostered teamwork and collaboration with fellow educators and the DLLs' families.

Chapter 8 highlights four more case studies showcasing specifically how teachers support the learning and development of DLLs with special needs:

- Tiffany Enciso-Williams (a former preschool special education teacher) reflected on the administrative support and professional

development needed for early childhood teachers to effectively work with culturally and linguistically diverse DLLs with special needs.
- Erin Vaccaro (a preschool-kindergarten special education teacher) described her applied behavior analysis strategies to work with a child with autism in a multiage, self-contained special education classroom.
- Lissette Ruiz (a prekindergarten teacher) shared her strategies in addressing the learning and developmental needs of three DLLs with special needs (one with autism spectrum disorder, one with delays in speech and cognitive processing, and another one with language impairments and challenging behaviors).
- Vanessa Casella (a former third-grade teacher) adapted her lessons to meet the special needs of her Spanish-English DLLs.

Reflective narratives in this book are presented as cases to capture certain contours of the complexities involved in teaching that may provide inspiration for other educators (e.g., early childhood pre-service and in-service teachers). Furthermore, these case narratives feature different age groups and early childhood grade levels to demonstrate the unique needs of culturally and linguistically diverse learners with different developmental and contextual characteristics. My hope is that the firsthand accounts of these cases by teacher narrators will convey real-life classroom scenarios that other educators may encounter or resonate with in their own work with young children.

In these case studies, the teachers as authors of their own voices are recognized by their actual names. However, to protect the identities of the children, their parents, and other educators in the case narratives, pseudonyms are used instead. NAEYC (2020) defined early childhood education as the provision of education to young children (ages birth through eight years or third grade). Accordingly, the term *early childhood educators* throughout this book refers to those who are working directly or indirectly with this age group of children, including caregivers/teachers in infant/toddler educational settings, center directors, teachers in preschool programs and early grades, and school administrators. Although this book focuses principally on DLLs, I recognize that some are multilingual/multicultural learners, mastering more than two languages. Together they constitute the growing population of culturally and linguistically diverse learners. By integrating and bridging theory with real-world applications in the classroom and drawing on early childhood teachers' voices as the practical foundation, I hope to empower other educators with relatable insights into the authentic world of teaching culturally and linguistically diverse learners, especially DLLs. Finally, this book concludes with chapter 9, presenting a successful recipe of responsive practice as involving both hard work and heart work.

Chapter Conclusion

This book represents a tapestry of theories interwoven with responsive practice through the authentic and candid voices of the early childhood teachers who shared their struggles, triumphs, challenges, and opportunities in working with culturally and linguistically diverse learners and their families. It is my hope that this book, grounded in the mindset of intentional responsiveness, will serve as a valuable resource for early childhood educators seeking to implement or refine their responsive practice with DLLs.

Reflection Questions

- Do you feel that you are given the opportunity and/or feel comfortable sharing your perspectives, triumphs, and struggles about your own teaching practice and student learning with others (e.g., school leaders, colleagues)?

- How might you use the teacher voices in this book to inform and/or inspire your own teaching?

- What does "reflective practice" mean to you?

- How have you engaged or might you engage in reflective practice?

- What is the Four Cornerstones of Responsive Practice framework about? What is its essential message?

- Why is it important to apply the Four Cornerstones of Responsive Practice framework in working with culturally and linguistically diverse learners?

CHAPTER 2

Reflective Practice

We do not learn from experience. We learn from reflection on experience.

—John Dewey, progressive and visionary American educator

In his seminal book *How We Think: A Restatement of the Relation of Reflective Thinking to the Educative Process*, John Dewey (1933) advocated that we reflect on our experience so that we may engage meaningfully in continuous learning and professional growth. Applying reflective practice as both a theoretical and practical framework, this book presents early childhood teachers' authentic voices reflecting on their teaching experiences. Particularly, their reflective narratives capture the challenges and opportunities they experienced as they engaged in developmentally, culturally, linguistically, and contextually responsive practice with DLLs in early childhood classrooms.

The Importance of Reflective Practice

Reflection is a necessary and critical recipe for responsive practice because through the reflective process, teachers can refine their teaching and further develop their professional expertise. In essence, *reflective practice* refers to a cognitive process that enables individuals to learn from their experiences by understanding what worked or did not work, why, and how, and then adjusting their practice accordingly (Chen 2022; Osterman and Kottkamp 2004). According to Dewey (1910, 1933), experiencing an unsettled mental state of mind, including doubts, confusion, and uncertainties, is a part of this reflective process that can lead to greater learning and professional growth. Furthermore, according to Donald Schön (1983, 1987), reflective practice also ensures that practitioners do not merely focus on applying a set of technical skills based on scientific knowledge, because this technical rationality approach only works in a "perfect" world where problems are unambiguous and where answers can be easily located. In this technical rationality case, the teachers are merely an instrument in finding the means to deliver a solution that is already determined. If everything fits robotically into place without any "messiness" of surprises and unexpected circumstances, the technical rationality of teaching should work—but it would be at the expense of developing and applying essential skills such as creativity and creative problem solving. Furthermore, it would also undermine the uniqueness of the competence and characteristics of the professionals. However, teaching is a highly complex endeavor that does not occur in a "perfect" world, and teachers are not mechanical robots performing routine work. Instead, teachers are influenced by the real social world, where many factors can affect how the teachers frame, understand, and interpret classroom situations. Thus, Dewey and Schön advocated a paradigm shift from technical rationality to a more reflective approach to better understand and refine our practices, thereby becoming "reflective practitioners."

The reflective approach is necessary for solving open-ended, nontechnical problems. Upon acquiring certain reflective skills, practitioners may apply these skills flexibly in their own practice to suit their professional needs and pivot their instruction accordingly. Thus, reflective practice is much needed to shift the paradigm from focusing on training teachers to enact certain teaching behaviors to empowering them with the ability and flexibility to analyze and understand why certain practices are effective and how they may apply them appropriately in context (e.g., aligning with educational goals, meeting diverse student learning needs). For example, teachers might reflect on how a certain strategy or theory was successful or unsuccessful in a particular teaching situation. The insights gleaned from such reflection could help teachers decide what modifications to make or actions to take to subsequently improve teaching and student learning. For instance, in my research study on reflective practice (Chen 2023, 336), one preschool teacher reflected on a teaching situation as follows:

> There were a couple math lessons that I had, where [the students] had to use Unifix cubes that I would have them measure different items in the classroom. So I would have them each go and pick an item, and then they would have to use Unifix cubes to measure. Some of those didn't go that well because they had a difficult time understanding that they have to stop stacking the cubes.... Sometimes the counting was difficult for them.... I realized that I probably should have done that as a small-group lesson rather than

a whole-group one. So then that's what I had done for the following lessons. I worked with them in small groups, which was definitely much better and it went well.

As the example above shows, reflection encourages educators to engage in reflective practice by thoughtfully identifying areas of strength and critically analyzing areas of weakness so they may seek to improve their teaching effectiveness and, by extension, enhance student learning outcomes. This process also encourages educators to set meaningful goals, create action plans, and implement evidence-based responsive practice accordingly. Furthermore, reflective practice should also compel educators to critically examine their own assumptions, biases, and preconceived notions about teaching and student learning, all of which can influence *what* and *how* they teach as well as *why* they teach the way they do. In essence, reflective practice can act as a catalyst for practitioners to learn and master their professional artistry.

Building on Dewey's idea about learning as related to reflection on experience, the case studies in this book invoke early childhood teachers' reflection on their teaching experiences with DLLs. It is important to note that reflection encompasses various types, including those occurring before teaching (reflection-for-action), during teaching (reflection-in-action), and after teaching (reflection-on-action). In this book, I focus only on the most commonly practiced type of reflection, namely *reflection-on-action*, or the process of thinking back on a teaching situation that has already occurred to learn from the experience and improve future practice or devise a plan for a follow-up action (Dewey 1910, 1933; Schön 1983, 1987). By engaging early childhood teachers in the process of reflecting-on-action, we can glean glimpses into the larger picture of their vital work with young children. Additionally, through reflection, teachers can develop the pedagogical adaptability that is so critical to becoming and being effective practitioners. Reflection promotes a continuous learning cycle by cultivating in teachers the capacity to engage in self-assessment and self-improvement in their teaching, thereby potentially contributing to their reflective practice.

Reflection as Key to Adaptive Expertise

In recent decades, teaching has been characterized as a "learning profession," where teachers learn to develop adaptive expertise (Darling-Lukemond and Sykes 1999). The term *adaptive expertise*, referred to as the effective application of knowledge in flexible manners, is described as the "gold standard for becoming a professional" (Hammerness et al. 2005, 360). Teachers who are considered adaptive experts characteristically leverage their available external resources in their environments and adapt to changing instructional expectations. They are also more likely to innovate their teaching rather than uncritically applying theoretical principles and engaging in prescribed practices.

The key to cultivating adaptive expertise is developing one's pedagogical adaptability, defined broadly as teachers' ability to adapt instructional practices effectively and constructively to teaching changes, demands, and challenges to address their students' diverse learning needs (Chen 2022). It is imperative that teachers develop pedagogical adaptability because when teachers are adaptive in using their knowledge of content, pedagogy, and student characteristics to meet the diverse needs of their learners (Chen, 2022; Vaughn, 2019), they are more likely to become and stay open-minded about possibilities and opportunities for improving their practice. For instance, they consider a variety of contextual factors in their teaching situation and are responsive to various needs of their students by differentiating, personalizing, and individualizing instructional content and learning activities (Chen 2016a). Vaughn (2019) found that the pedagogical adaptations commonly shared across teachers included modeling a skill, providing an example, offering a new perspective to students, and changing group assignments. Given the importance of reflection, other strategies promoting pedagogical adaptability may include encouraging educators to engage in thoughtful and continuous reflection about unexpected changes and challenges from which to develop effective adaptive strategies (Chen 2022).

How Should Teachers Reflect-on-Action?

It is well established that pedagogical adaptability is an essential archetype of effective practice that teachers should emulate (Chen 2023; Vaughn 2019). However, pedagogical adaptability does not occur in a vacuum. One effective means to develop pedagogical adaptability is through intentional teacher reflection. Teachers might have already learned from their teacher preparation programs about reflection and the process of engaging in reflection as a necessary catalyst for teaching refinement. However, there exists a difference between learning about reflection and fully understanding and wholeheartedly implementing reflection as an essential disposition and skill in educators' professional development.

To develop and integrate reflection as a professional disposition and skill into one's teaching work, the educator should understand that reflection is an active cognitive process. For example, when teachers engage in critical reflection-on-action, they question *why* and *how* they make certain decisions and engage in certain teaching behaviors to solve certain teaching problems or situations. In doing so, reflection "emancipates us from merely impulsive and merely routine activity" (Dewey 1933, 17). The big question still remains: *How should educators reflect-on-action?* As a starter, teachers seeking to engage in reflective practice should ask themselves questions to guide their reflection. These questions may include the following:

1. What specific lesson/topic did I teach?
2. What method/strategy did I use to teach the lesson/topic?
3. What student learning outcomes did I expect to happen?
4. How did I assess whether these student learning outcomes were met or not?
5. What went well and what did not go as well as expected? And why?
6. What did I learn from what went well or what did not go well?
7. What could I do about what did not go well?
8. Did my lesson meet the children's diverse developmental, cultural, linguistic, and contextual learning strengths and needs? If not, why not, and what could I do about it?

These questions can help spark the teachers' self-introspection. Through this process, they may achieve a deeper level of understanding of themselves as teachers and learners. Additionally, teachers may deepen their awareness of their own teaching practice as well as the teaching-learning context and outcomes. Furthermore, a major benefit derived from teacher reflection is teacher development. For instance, by engaging in reflection, teachers can gain an increased understanding of the successes, setbacks, challenges, and opportunities they encountered in the field. This knowledge can, in turn, help guide them in improving their own practices in the future, thereby enabling them to grow into more competent and confident professionals as they continue working in the context of the ever-increasing diverse student populations.

Chapter Conclusion

It is clear that reflective practice is critical to helping practitioners become effective. Teaching practices that are premised on reflection lay a solid foundation for informing, affirming, transforming, and reforming one's teaching.

Furthermore, reflection can serve as a driving force for educators to develop adaptive expertise and related pedagogical adaptability. Thus, by engaging in reflective practice, teachers may become more effective in supporting the learning and development of all children, especially DLLs. To guide the process of reflection, teachers can start asking themselves probing questions related to a particular lesson that may spark new ideas for improving certain aspects of their teaching practice.

Reflection Questions

- What does reflective practice mean to you?
- What has prompted or might prompt you to reflect on your teaching practice?
- How have you engaged or how might you engage in reflective practice?
- How have you integrated or how might you integrate reflective practice as an essential aspect of your professional development?
- How have you integrated or how might you integrate reflection as a routine teaching practice?

CHAPTER 3

Increasing Superdiversity

We become not a melting pot but a beautiful mosaic. Different people, different beliefs, different yearnings, different hopes, different dreams.

—Jimmy Carter, former US president

The above quote, attributed to President Jimmy Carter, is believed to have been said in 1976 during his presidential debate. By this quote, Carter acknowledges the unique contributions and diverse experiences of all people in the United States as giving rise to a "beautiful mosaic" that deserves celebration and preservation. This portrayal reflects the United States as a nation comprised of immigrants from diverse regions around the globe. Notably, President John F. Kennedy referred to the United States as "a nation of immigrants," which was the title of his book, posthumously published in 1964. This book was based on a series of essays and speeches that he delivered on the history, evolution, contributions, and experiences of immigrants in the United States.

According to the latest report by the Migration Policy Institute (2024), as of 2022, there were more than 46 million immigrants in the United States, who constituted 13.9 percent of the overall US population. Historically, the United States was once characterized as a "melting pot," suggesting that diverse cultural groups of immigrants were melded together as one homogeneous whole. This phenomenon was prevalent especially during a period known as the "great wave" of immigration in the late nineteenth and early twentieth centuries, with a significant influx of immigrants from northwestern Europe (notably Ireland and Germany). More saliently, the melting pot metaphor gained popularity in the United States through a 1908 play appropriately titled *The Melting Pot* by Israel Zangwill. The melting pot has since drawn concern from critics, such as Henry Pratt Fairchild (1926), Philip Gleason (1964), and Charles Hirschman (1983). These critics are concerned that the melting pot model promotes the homogenization and assimilation of diverse cultural groups into a singular dominant culture at the expense of recognizing and respecting diverse cultural identities. Instead, they advocate for more inclusive and pluralistic depictions, such as the "salad bowl" and "cultural mosaic," which emphasize the coexistence of diverse cultures. These modern characterizations encourage the preservation of distinct cultural identities and recognize the unique contributions that different cultural groups bring to create the rich tapestry of American society.

Since the early twentieth century, demographic trends have expanded immigration beyond northwestern Europe to include immigrants from a wider constellation of regions worldwide. To capture and honor the complexities, richness, and distinct contributions of the diverse cultures brought along by immigrants, German-born American philosopher Horace Kallen (1915) coined the term "cultural pluralism." In a more contemporary discourse, scholars (e.g., Bruce Fuller 2003; William Hazard and Madelon Stent 1973) have also increasingly discussed the perspective of "cultural pluralism" in the context of education and education policy.

The sociodemographic characteristics of the US population are constantly changing. Suffice it to say that one of the major drivers is immigration. Reflecting these sociodemographic trends, the United States is home to immigrants from many different countries and cultures. In recent years, it has also increasingly become a superdiverse country characterized by high levels of diversity *within* culturally, linguistically, socioeconomically, and/or racially/ethnically distinct groups, not just *across* groups. The term *diversity* may be defined as the existence of people from a wide variety of backgrounds (including cultural, linguistic, and socioeconomic). The term *superdiversity* was introduced by Steven Vertovec in 2007 to characterize the nature of immigration to Britain as exhibiting substantially higher levels of population diversity than before, especially with respect to the immigrant and ethnic minority population. In the literature, *superdiversity* appears to be used interchangeably with the term *hyperdiversity*. David Hollinger (1995) described superdiversity as "diversification of diversity." Furthermore, the phenomenon of superdiversity depicts not only the growing diversity between and within immigrant and ethnic minority groups but also the proliferation of additional variables (beyond the obvious racial/ethnic profiles and countries of origin) that include distinct immigration statuses as well as gender and age characteristics (Vertovec 2007). In sum, it is essentially through the intricate interplay of these various critical factors that the immigrant population has become more diverse than ever.

Superdiversity in Languages Spoken in the United States

While the United States as a whole is generally considered superdiverse, the nature and extent of superdiversity actually vary across the states within the country. The nature of superdiversity is evident especially when using language as a proxy. According to their analysis of the US Census Bureau data from the 2019 American Community Survey, Sandy Dietrich and Erik Hernandez (2022) reported that the number of individuals in the United States who spoke a language other than English in their households had nearly tripled from 23.1 million (about one in ten) in 1980 to 67.8 million (nearly one in five) in 2019. As reported by the US Census Bureau in 2015, at least 350 other languages, including Indigenous languages, were spoken in the United States. However, not all of these languages were found within one state. In fact, the linguistic diversity varied across states, with the greatest number of languages (192) spoken in the New York metro area, followed by the Los Angeles metro area (185) (Dietrich and Hernandez 2022). Take Spanish, for example: according to an analysis of census data by Maki Park and colleagues (2018), the prevalence of Spanish-speaking households varied among states, with the highest percentages found in Texas (78 percent), New Mexico (71 percent), and Arizona (71 percent), and the lowest percentages in Vermont (16 percent) and Maine (16 percent). Beyond Spanish, other languages were also concentrated differently across the states. Noticeably, Chinese was the second most-spoken language among the parents of DLLs in ten states, including California and New York, while Arabic was the second most common language in four states, including Michigan and Virginia, and Hmong was the second most frequently spoken language in two states (Minnesota and Wisconsin) (Park, Zong, and Batalova 2018).

Superdiversity among Young Learners in the United States

On the first day of school, Mrs. Adler welcomes twenty culturally and linguistically diverse learners into her first-grade classroom in an urban school that serves children from low-income backgrounds:

- Marabella (who just arrived in the United States from Ecuador two months ago) speaks fluent Spanish at home but knows no English.
- Victor (who was born in the United States to Mexican immigrant parents) speaks some Spanish and some English, and exhibits challenging behaviors.

- *Ling Ling (who immigrated to the United States with his family from China a year ago) speaks fluent Mandarin Chinese at home but communicates in English with hesitation and some difficulty.*
- *Harman (an American-born Indian) speaks some Hindi but prefers to use English.*
- *Lilian (who was adopted from Korea when she was an infant by an ethnically mixed Korean and White family) understands some Korean but speaks English fluently.*
- *Antonio (who immigrated from Portugal with his family two years ago) is diagnosed with speech delays in both Portuguese and English and requires special education services.*
- *The rest of the children come from other cultural and linguistic backgrounds with unique learning abilities and needs.*

This superdiverse composition of learners with unique cultural and linguistic characteristics within and between them in one classroom is not unusual, especially in an urban school in the United States. It is also not uncommon to find that many of these learners are DLLs. According to the 2011–2015 American Community Survey, there were more than 11.5 million DLLs between the ages of birth to eight, constituting nearly one-third of the 36.3 million children in this age range. They represented a large increase from one-quarter in 2000, thereby making DLLs the fastest-growing child population in the country (Park, Zong, and Batalova 2018).

Not surprisingly, immigration has become the biggest contributor to the increasing DLL population in the United States. Maki Park and colleagues (2018) found that many parents of DLLs were immigrants, as were some DLLs themselves. For instance, of the 12.8 million parents of DLLs across the nation, 65 percent are immigrants and more than one-quarter of these immigrants are new arrivals to the United States within the last decade (with Indian, Chinese, and other Asian-born parents being large contributors of immigrant parents). In turn, the continuous influxes of immigrants from other countries have naturally contributed to the increasing cultural and linguistic diversity and superdiversity associated with the prominent presence of DLLs in early childhood settings across the United States (Chen 2016a).

Factors Contributing to Superdiversity

Notwithstanding their large collective presence in the United States, DLLs are not a monolithic, homogeneous group but rather vary in many respects. Park and colleagues (2018) adopted the term *superdiversity* to refer to the growing diversity within and across communities in the United States as measured by several factors, especially languages spoken, race and ethnicity, and countries of origin. Specifically, they elucidated these factors with statistical data as summarized below:

- **Languages spoken.** More than 90 percent of the parents of DLLs spoke a home language other than English, with Spanish being the most prevalent non-English language, spoken by 59 percent of the parents in 2011–2015 across nearly all states. This is not surprising given that the largest sources (51 percent) of all immigrants were Mexico and other Latin American countries. What was also noteworthy is that Spanish was spoken by twelve times as many people as the next frequently spoken language, namely, Chinese, which accounted for only 5.2 percent of the language minority population. More specifically, Chinese was spoken by 3 percent of the DLLs' parents. After Spanish and Chinese, the next dominant languages spoken in the homes of DLLs were Tagalog, Vietnamese, and Arabic (each spoken by 2 percent of DLLs' parents).
- **Race and ethnicity.** Most DLLs (62 percent) were Hispanic, followed by 16 percent White, 15 percent Asian, 6 percent Black, and 1 percent American Indian.
- **Countries of origin.** While 65 percent of the parents of DLLs were immigrants, most DLLs (95 percent) were actually born in the United States. However, among the top sources of parents of DLLs, 41 percent were from Mexico, followed by 7 percent from India, 4 percent from El Salvador, and 3 percent each from China and the Philippines.

Differences in Family Backgrounds between DLLs and Non-DLLs

Families of DLLs tend to vary from families of non-DLLs in certain ways, especially family structure, income levels, parents' educational attainment, and parents' English proficiency, as summarized from Park and colleagues' (2018) analyses below:

- **Intact two-parent family structure.** There were more DLLs (77 percent) living in intact two-parent families than their non-DLL counterparts (69 percent).
- **Family income.** Overall, DLLs exhibited greater vulnerability to poverty, as 31 percent of them resided in families with incomes below the federal poverty level, compared to 22 percent of their non-DLL counterparts. Another noticeable marker of DLLs' lower family income levels was their enrollment in Head Start programs serving children from low-income backgrounds. In particular, as of this writing, the Head Start program's latest fact sheets reported that during the 2021–2022 program year, Head Start programs collectively served 801,859 children (ages birth to five years), of whom 33 percent were DLLs (US Department of Health and Human Services and Administration for Children and Families, 2023).
- **Educational attainment.** DLLs' parents were likely to have less education compared to non-DLL parents, with 26 percent of DLL's parents attaining less than a high school diploma compared to 6 percent of parents of non-DLLs.
- **Linguistic isolation.** Nearly a quarter (24 percent) of DLLs experienced linguistic isolation due to their family members having limited or no English proficiency. Consequently, these DLLs tended to encounter limited access to critical educational, medical, and other services.

As Park and colleagues (2018) emphasized, while these statistics painted a collective portrait of the DLL population, there was embedded superdiversity not only between and within the various DLL groups, but also within and across the states in the United States. In the United States, the education systems and policies are not centralized but implemented, managed, and monitored at state and local levels. Thus, while overall, some states do not seem to be superdiverse, they can still have counties and school districts that exhibit superdiversity.

Evidence of Superdiversity within DLLs and the Influences of Home Factors

The superdiversity phenomenon reinforces the idea that DLLs are not a homogenous group. Even within the same cultural group, there is great diversity. For instance, in our study of eighty-four Chinese-English preschool DLLs, a seemingly homogenous group (all from immigrant, low-income backgrounds), we (Chen and Ren 2019) found that they actually varied in bilingual language and literacy practices, giving rise to three distinct groups: (1) Chinese-dominant children who read only in Chinese, (2) English-dominant children who read solely in English, and (3) bilingual language–dominant children who read in both Chinese and English. We also found that the language used by the parents to interact with their children influenced these children's bilingual development. For instance, DLLs whose parents read to them solely in Chinese (Chinese-dominant) and those whose parents read to them in both Chinese and English (bilingual language–dominant) scored higher in receptive Chinese than those whose parents did not read to them in any language. Furthermore, children whose parents conversed with them in both English and Chinese (bilingual language–dominant) performed better in expressive English than those whose parents interacted with them exclusively in Chinese (Chinese-dominant). These findings suggest that the linguistic backgrounds and practices within DLL families encompass a wide spectrum, as reflected in both the qualitative (*how*) and quantitative (*how much*) exposure to a particular language by the DLLs in the home.

In addition to language exposure at home, children's language learning in their previous schooling plays a crucial role in determining their success in language acquisition (Chen 2016a; Collier and Thomas 2017). For instance, compared to a peer who has not had any formal education in their home language, a child who has had schooling in their home language may be better able to maintain this language while learning English in a US school setting. Furthermore, cultural exposure is crucial in motivating DLLs to acquire their home language. As language and culture are intricately linked, engaging in cultural activities and community participation can foster DLL's home language development.

Risk and Protective Factors Influencing DLLs' Educational Experiences

As discussed previously, the evolving demographics, which contribute to the ever-expanding DLL population, have also transformed the landscape of the US education system into a vibrant tapestry of diversity. In turn, the superdiversity in early childhood settings presents both challenges and opportunities for early childhood educators as they work with DLLs who have a wide range of diverse characteristics within and between them. Thus, educators need to understand the risk and protective factors that can affect the quality of DLLs' educational experiences so that they can support these children's learning and developmental needs accordingly. Here are three potential risk factors:

- **The urban disadvantage in resource and educational quality.** Students attending urban schools are more likely to receive insufficient educational resources and low-quality education (Sandy and Duncan 2010). This may be because urban schools tend to have more concentrated poverty (West 2007).
- **The disproportionately low socioeconomic status (SES) among minority students.** Schools with a high concentration of minority students often have low SES backgrounds (Kenty-Drane 2009).
- **The low SES disadvantage in educational achievement.** There are educational achievement disparities between students from low SES backgrounds and those from high SES backgrounds, with the former having lower levels of academic performance (West 2007). Specifically, students eligible for free or reduced-price lunch (used as a proxy for the school's SES) tend to score lower in reading and math performances compared to those who are not eligible (Borg, Borg, and Stranahan 2012).

DLLs who are minorities, come from low-income backgrounds, and attend school in urban educational settings are likely confronted with the aforementioned contextual challenges that can affect their academic success. The achievement gap between DLLs and their monolingual English-speaking counterparts is real, even after these DLLs have been educated for five or six years in the US education system (Ballantyne, Sanderman, and McLaughlin 2008).

While there may be risk factors thwarting the educational progress of DLLs, protective factors may buffer them against these adverse effects. Here are two potential protective factors:

- **The value of home language and culture.** There are great benefits for DLLs to acquire and maintain their home language. Most importantly, by using their home language, DLLs can build relationships and strengthen bonds with their family members (particularly parents and grandparents) and other members of their ethnic community who primarily communicate in their home language. Furthermore, DLLs' home language serves as an invaluable gateway to their ancestral heritage, allowing them to learn about and connect with their native culture on a profound level. For example, proficiency in their home language empowers children to use language to explore their cultural roots, traditions, and values through interactions with cultural

artifacts and members of their ethnic community (Chen 2016a; Erdosi and Chen 2023).
- **The advantage of positive transfer in bilingualism/ multilingualism.** DLLs can transfer their communicative and cognitive skills from one language to another to enhance their language learning (Chen 2016a).

These protective factors and the like can motivate DLLs to foster their bilingual abilities. They also serve as strong reasons for why educational approaches should embrace and capitalize on DLLs' language and cultural strengths to support their learning and developmental needs.

Implications of Superdiversity for Supporting DLLs

The DLLs are more than meets the eye, as there is superdiversity within and across this population. DLLs' families speak many different languages, come from many countries of origin, and have distinct racial and ethnic backgrounds, socioeconomic statuses, educational levels, immigration histories, and other unique characteristics, all of which make them superdiverse (Park, Zong, and Batalova 2018). Such superdiversity is manifested in many early childhood classrooms throughout the country. In turn, they present both challenges and opportunities for the education system and the teachers to better work with DLLs.

The traditional educational approach to serving DLLs' learning and developmental needs is through bilingual education. However, this strategy works only if the two target languages of learning meet the DLLs' linguistic needs. Within the superdiversity found in early childhood classrooms, where many non-English languages are spoken and multiple cultures are represented, bilingual education services cannot address all multilinguistic and multicultural needs of young children (Park, Zong, and Batalova 2018). This phenomenon suggests that no one-size-fits-all solution would suffice, especially as the DLL population continues to diversify. Nonetheless, the teachers' responsiveness to DLLs' developmental, cultural, linguistic, and contextual circumstances is key to begin meeting their learning needs. For instance, teachers can empower DLLs to navigate between their home and the school environment successfully by promoting DLLs' home language and culture as strengths in classroom activities (Chen 2016a). It is not surprising then to find that when their home language is valued, DLLs communicate effectively in both their home language and English during learning activities, such as dramatic play (Chen and Kacerek 2022).

Given the superdiversity among DLLs, teachers must be equipped with appropriate knowledge, skills, and dispositions to effectively teach this diverse population within their classrooms that may often be multicultural and multilingual. Chapters 6–8 provide authentic examples of how teachers address the challenges and opportunities presented to them in their vital work with DLLs. Their reflective narratives highlight the importance of establishing a support system for DLLs to thrive.

Chapter Conclusion

The growing superdiversity among DLLs means they have been and will continue to represent a heterogeneous group. They bring to the classroom their own unique cultural and linguistic strengths and needs. Thus, it is imperative that early childhood educators apply a superdiversity lens to critically assess the learning and development of their DLLs and provide responsive support accordingly. In theory, supporting bilingual and biliteracy development in DLLs may seem like a no-brainer. In practice, it requires applying the Four Cornerstones of Responsive Practice framework that considers their dynamic developmental, cultural, linguistic, and contextual needs. This practice is especially important because DLLs are a heterogeneous group that is superdiverse in their background characteristics, such as race/ethnicity, country of origin, parents' educational levels and SES, and home language exposure.

Reflection Questions

- Have you noticed superdiversity in your classroom or someone else's classroom? If so, what does superdiversity look like in the classroom?

- How have or how might you adapt your teaching strategies that consider the superdiversity of students in your classroom?

- How have you utilized or how might you utilize your knowledge about superdiversity to better facilitate DLLs' learning and development? For example, what specific developmental, cultural, linguistic, and contextual factors have you considered or might you consider when supporting DLLs' learning and development?

CHAPTER 4

Language Skills: Receptive, Expressive, BICS, and CALP

A special kind of beauty exists which is born in language, of language, and for language.

—Gaston Bachelard, French philosopher and writer

Gaston Bachelard recognizes a unique and profound kind of beauty derived fundamentally from language itself, connected intimately to the art of language, and appreciated or communicated intricately through language. In essence, Bachelard establishes the power of language in yielding and connecting to such inherent beauty. The corollary is that to experience such beauty, language acquisition is key. However, acquiring a language, let alone multiple languages, is not a straightforward process but a dynamic, complex one that requires instructional support such as the framework advocated in this book—the Four Cornerstones of Responsive Practice.

To engage in responsive practice, it is imperative that early childhood teachers understand the key language skills needed for children to interact socially with others and succeed academically. In this chapter, I highlight specifically four types of language skills: (1) receptive, (2) expressive, (3) basic interpersonal communicative skills (BICS), and (4) cognitive academic language proficiency (CALP). The latter two specific language skills were proposed by second-language acquisition expert Jim Cummins (1979). All four language skills are distinct yet interconnected to inform the learner's abilities in social and academic communication and success.

Receptive and Expressive Language Skills

Proficiency in language skills (speaking, listening, reading, and writing) is essential for effective communication and success in school and beyond. In the early stages of language development, before they have acquired sufficient language proficiency, children often rely on nonverbal methods, such as hand gestures, facial expressions, and visual cues, to communicate their needs, wants, feelings, and thoughts. Young children develop two critical yet distinct aspects of language skills: (1) receptive language and (2) expressive language.

Receptive language refers generally to the ability to understand language by processing and interpreting spoken words, gestures, and other forms of communication conveyed by others. It encompasses listening comprehension (what is being said orally) and reading comprehension (what is being communicated in writing or sign language). For instance, when the teacher speaks or reads a book to the children in the classroom, the children rely on receptive language skills to decode and comprehend the spoken words, sentences, and overall message. They may also rely on other receptive language skills by understanding and interpreting the teacher's nonverbal cues, such as vocal tone, facial expressions, and body language.

Expressive language refers generally to the ability to generate language by appropriately conveying such cues as one's needs, wants, feelings, and thoughts. It encompasses oral (speaking using words), writing or sign language, and nonverbal forms (using facial expressions, gestures, body language, and visual aids). For example, when the teacher and children speak, write, or use nonverbal cues, they utilize their expressive language skills to communicate.

Receptive and expressive language skills are two different yet interrelated sets of language skills that are both essential for effective communication. I highlight specifically four features concerning their nature and relationships in the process of language development:

- **The complementary nature of receptive and expressive language skills.** Receptive language skills (involving the ability to comprehend spoken, written, or sign language) and expressive language skills (entailing the ability to express oneself using spoken, written, or sign language) are complementary, and together they can facilitate effective communication. The relationship between receptive and expressive language has been documented by research such as that by Evelyn Fisher (2017). For instance, when listening to a story being read aloud by the teacher, a child processes the spoken language he hears and thereby practices receptive language skills. He then shows

his comprehension of the storyline by answering questions about it. In the process, he applies his receptive language of understanding the storyline to help convey his ideas to show his expressive language ability. Furthermore, as children advance in their language development, a reciprocal relationship between receptive language skills and expressive language skills can be seen. They are mutually reinforcing in such a way that a strong foundation in one can support the acquisition of the other as children engage in the process of developing one or more languages. For example, when children develop their receptive language skills by building vocabulary and understanding how words, sentences, and grammar function, they can better incorporate these elements in generating and expressing their own coherent and meaningful speech and writing. Furthermore, receptive language skills and expressive language skills are used in understanding the syntactic (the grammatical structure and rules of a sentence) and semantic (the meanings of words, phrases, and symbols) aspects of language. In addition, receptive language skills also facilitate the understanding of the pragmatic functions of a language, meaning the ways in which the context affects the interpretation, understanding, and communication of the conveyed message. This knowledge is essential to children's appropriate and effective use of language to understand and express themselves in communication with others in different social contexts.
- **The developmental sequence of language acquisition.** In the typical developmental sequence of acquisition in the first (L1) or second (L2) language, children's receptive language skills generally precede their expressive language skills. As seen in infants and young children, in the beginning, they usually understand more words than they can express. That is, they first learn to grasp and interpret some language before they begin producing any.
- **The assessment of DLLs' receptive and expressive language skills in both their home language(s) and English.** In the context of the bilingual/multilingual development of DLLs, early childhood teachers should assess these children's receptive and expressive language abilities in both their home language(s) and in English to better support their development in these languages and empower them to become effective communicators using either language (Chen and Ren 2019). Furthermore, early childhood teachers should also conduct language observations and assessments in both receptive and expressive

language skills through which they may identify potential language disorders or delays in DLLs to make necessary referrals for further evaluation. In the case of DLLs with suspected language disorders or delays, evaluation should then be conducted in both their L1 and L2 to gain more comprehensive insights into their language areas of concern.

- **The receptive and expressive language abilities in children with language conditions.** The typical developmental sequence involving generally the acquisition of some receptive language skills before expressive language skills and the reciprocal relationship between the two may not apply to cases of language disorders or delays (Rezvan et al. 2024). For instance, children, including DLLs, with language disorders or delays may have an imbalanced development of receptive and expressive language skills in such a way that they may be stronger in the receptive area than the expressive area or vice versa. If diagnosed with a language disorder or speech delay, these children may receive early intervention of special services to target support in identified areas. In such a case, professionals, especially speech pathologists, can work with these children to improve their language skills accordingly to help them achieve better communication abilities.

Basic Interpersonal Communicative Skills and Cognitive Academic Language Proficiency

In addition to receptive and expressive language skills, children are developing two other types, which Jim Cummins (1979, 1980) termed *basic interpersonal communicative skills* (BICS) and *cognitive academic language proficiency* (CALP). A fundamental difference between BICS and CALP lies in their contextualized/decontextualized nature. Cummins defined BICS as the language skills needed for conversational fluency in everyday social interactions and CALP as the language skills needed in academic settings. BICS is highly contextualized because it involves the use of simple, here-and-now support (including verbal cues, facial expressions and gestures, visuals, and concrete objects) to communicate effectively with others. In contrast, CALP is highly decontextualized, with high levels of cognitive demands. Specifically, it involves utilizing specialized academic language (such as specific vocabulary and complex sentence structures) to grasp and articulate one's understanding of abstract concepts and complex ideas (including analyzing decontextualized information and participating in academic discussions). It also invokes a repertoire of high-level literacy (reading and writing)

4 | Language Skills: Receptive, Expressive, BICS, and CALP

skills as well as the application of cultural nuances. In essence, CALP is known as the language of academic success, especially given that the academic content in most subject areas uses context-reduced or decontextualized language. Thus, CALP is considered a major factor in determining the academic success of all students in early grades and beyond.

Due to the different natures of BICS and CALP in cognitive demands, children tend to acquire BICS quicker and easier than CALP. Based on his work with second language learners, Cummins (1979, 1980) confirmed that it may take these learners anytime within two years to acquire BICS, but five to seven years or even longer to develop CALP. Mastering CALP is challenging enough for all children; it is especially so for those DLLs who are not yet proficient in understanding and using academic language in English. For instance, with few or no context clues, listening to a teacher read a storybook can pose a significant hurdle to these DLLs as they struggle to comprehend the many unfamiliar words or new concepts expressed in the text. Consequently, they may not be able to understand the story or articulate their understanding of it. Nonetheless, as academic language is used in formal school settings, it is imperative that DLLs acquire CALP to become and stay academically successful. Educators are in a unique position to scaffold DLLs' CALP in English while sensibly supporting the maintenance of their home language and culture.

Supporting Positive Transfer of Skills from One Language to Another

Theoretical and empirical evidence corroborates the benefits of bilingualism. In particular, Cummins's (1981) concept of the *common underlying proficiency* (CUP) is commonly used in the field of bilingual education and second language acquisition. It refers to the individuals' shared cognitive and linguistic proficiencies across two or more languages. Cummins (1981) further proposed the "interdependence hypothesis" in relation to positive transfer of skills from one language to another, highlighting the importance of language exposure and instruction as follows: "To the extent that instruction in Lx is effective in promoting proficiency in Lx, transfer of this proficiency to Ly will occur provided there is adequate exposure to Ly (either in school or environment) and adequate motivation to learn Ly" (29). By virtue of CUP and the interdependence hypothesis, when individuals learn one language, their cognitive ability and proficiency skills in this language can help them learn another language more effectively and easily. In other words, the cognitive and linguistic skills acquired in one language can potentially transfer to and benefit the learning of another language. For instance, if children are already proficient in their native language, they have already established a strong foundation in this language in skills such as vocabulary building and grammatical structures. This foundation can, in turn, help the child acquire a second or additional language more easily. Thus, we should leverage CUP to encourage DLLs to continue developing and maintaining their home language while helping them to simultaneously acquire English in school.

The illustration of Cummins's proposed CUP theory may be likened to an "iceberg" structure (see figure 1), suggesting that while L1 and L2 have distinct surface features, they are not isolated abilities but rather share proficiencies. That is, at a deeper level, there exist fundamental commonalities linking the two languages. Thus, any growth in CUP in one language will potentially render a beneficial effect on the other.

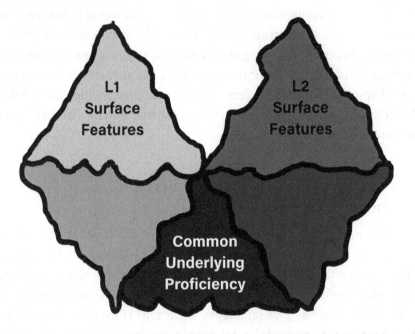

Figure 1. The iceberg model represents Cummins's (1981) common underlying proficiency theory.

As Cummins (2000, 39) further emphasized, "Conceptual knowledge developed in one language helps to make input in the other language comprehensible." For instance, as Spanish and English have many cognates or near-cognates (such as *idea*, *lava*, and *animal*, in both English and Spanish, or *garden* in English and *garten* in Spanish), understanding the meanings and even spellings of these cognates in one language can help someone understand them in the other language. There may also be positive transfer of grammar rules from one language to another that can facilitate bilingual and biliteracy development. Research corroborates that bilingual instruction guided by CUP can contribute to literacy-related skills and academic outcomes, especially in the two languages of Spanish and English, making learning English easier for Spanish speakers (e.g., Cheung and Slavin 2012; Farver, Lonigan, and Eppe 2009).

Educators should also note that there may also be negative transfer of knowledge and skills between two languages. For instance, in Mandarin Chinese, general nouns are used typically without any definite and indefinite articles—that is, *the* and *a/an* in English (Chen 2016b). In this case, when a Chinese-English DLL attempts to apply this Chinese rule, it can result in negative transfer, such as saying, "I went to store," instead of "I went to the store." In this case, the omission of the article *the* is considered grammatically correct in Chinese but not so in English.

The Benefits of Bilingual Education for DLLs' Language Development

As research evidence substantiates, bilingual education can contribute to a well-rounded education that prepares students for success in the academic domain and later in life in an increasingly diverse global world. For instance, my synthesis of the research on dual language immersion (also known as two-way immersion and bilingual immersion) attests to the positive effect of bilingual instruction on bilingual children's academic achievement (Chen 2014). Thomas and Collier (2002) also found that after four to seven years of immersion in bilingual education, bilingual students in K–12 settings in the United States consistently outperformed their monolingually educated peers across all subjects. Furthermore, drawing from thirty-two years of research encompassing longitudinal studies involving 7.5 million English learners across all language backgrounds in grades K–12 in thirty-six school districts across sixteen US states, Collier and Thomas (2017) found that English-only and transitional bilingual programs implemented for a short duration only partially closed about half of the achievement gap between English learners and their native English-speaking peers. Conversely, high-quality, long-term bilingual programs proved effective in closing all gaps after five to six years of bilingual education. Collier and Thomas further concluded that it takes, on average, six years for English language learners starting in kindergarten and receiving quality bilingual schooling in both their L1 and L2 to reach grade-level competence in L2 and stay at or above grade level throughout the rest of their schooling. However, this estimation can vary across learners depending on a host of factors, including the quality and quantity of instruction in their L1 and L2.

The previous research findings highlight the positive impact of bilingual education on the academic success of English language learners. However, while bilingual education seems ideal for DLLs to achieve proficiency in two languages, it is not always possible to offer bilingual education, given the superdiversity in the classroom (as discussed in chapter 2). Furthermore, political opinions on bilingual education and budgetary allowances can influence decisions on which types of educational programs to offer DLLs to support their language learning and academic success. Nonetheless, in all classrooms (monolingual or bilingual), it is imperative that we design a learning environment that promotes bilingual acquisition (to the extent possible) as key to social and academic success for DLLs.

Chapter Conclusion

As DLLs are learning English while maintaining their home language(s), they need to acquire specific language skills, especially receptive language, expressive language, BICS, and CALP to succeed socially and academically and communicate effectively in school and beyond. Although receptive language and expressive language are distinct, as the former relates to comprehending language input and the latter to conveying language output, both are foundational for effective social and academic communication. Furthermore, BICS and CALP are also needed for achieving social and academic success, respectively. The importance of the four language skills (receptive, expressive, BICS, and CALP) discussed in this chapter urges early childhood educators to devise strategies to better scaffold DLLs in attaining success in both social and academic contexts.

Reflection Questions

- How have you supported or how might you support the acquisition of the four language skills (receptive, expressive, BICS, and CALP) in children, especially DLLs?

- What strategies have you found or might you find effective in scaffolding the acquisition of these different language skills in children, especially DLLs? How are these strategies effective?

- Have you found any strategies that are not effective with DLLs? What are they? Why are they not effective?

CHAPTER 5

The Four Cornerstones of Responsive Practice Framework

Developmentally appropriate practice does not mean a single "best" practice.

Rather, it emphasizes a dynamic and complex set of practices that respect, value, and build on the varied strengths children and their families bring to the educational process. It encompasses the understanding that the social, cultural, linguistic, and historical contexts in which children, their families, and teachers live and work have a tremendous influence on these children's development and learning.

—Jennifer J. Chen and Dana Battaglia

In the introduction to NAEYC's *Casebook: Developmentally Appropriate Practice in Early Childhood Programs Serving Children from Birth through Age 8* (Brillante et al. 2023), Dana Battaglia and I emphasized the interplay between development and contextual factors, including social, cultural, and linguistic influences. Development cannot be understood in isolation from its context. Thus, when it comes to understanding and scaffolding the development of children, especially DLLs, it is essential that early childhood educators recognize and consider the specific context in which these children live, learn, and grow (Chen and Battaglia 2023). Likewise, effective practices must consider the unique cultural backgrounds, linguistic environments, and other contextual dynamics that shape each child's developmental outcomes.

Given the increasing superdiversity (as discussed in chapter 3) existing in many early childhood classrooms serving young DLLs (from birth to age eight or third grade) throughout the United States, it is particularly imperative that we have a responsive framework to guide practice. In this connection, I put forward the Four Cornerstones of Responsive Practice as both a theoretical and practical framework (see figure 2), in which the child is positioned as the focal point interlocking with four core parts of the whole: (1) developmentally responsive practice, (2) culturally responsive practice, (3) linguistically responsive practice, and (4) contextually responsive practice. The Four Cornerstones of Responsive Practice framework symbolizes the foundation on which responsive practice is built and supported. It is worth noting that this framework represents a collective and not a singular "best" practice. Accordingly, it comprises an array of practices that are responsive to the developmental, cultural, linguistic, and contextual needs of the children. Furthermore, this idea builds upon the developmentally appropriate practice framework established by NAEYC. It also draws on the 3CAPs framework put forward by Hui Li and me (Li and Chen 2017): (1) culturally appropriate practice, (2) contextually appropriate practice, and (3) child-individually appropriate practice.

NAEYC's latest position statement (2020) emphasized developmentally appropriate practice as reflecting three essential and interrelated elements: (1) three core considerations (commonality, individuality, and context) that guide the educators' decision-making, (2) nine principles of child development and learning (e.g., child centered, play based, constructivist oriented) that inform practice, and (3) six guidelines for professional practice. In particular, the six critical practical guidelines encompass "(1) creating a caring community of learners; (2) engaging in reciprocal partnerships with families and fostering community connections; (3) observing, documenting and assessing children's development and learning; (4) teaching to enhance each child's development and learning; (5) planning and implementing an engaging curriculum to achieve meaningful goals; and (6) demonstrating professionalism as an early childhood educator" (NAEYC 2020, 14). Collectively, these core considerations, principles, and guidelines serve as the foundation of developmentally appropriate practice.

My Four Cornerstones of Responsive Practice framework offers further clarity to the understanding and application of developmentally appropriate practice, ensuring that responsive practice aligns specifically with the distinctive yet interwoven dimensions (developmental, cultural, linguistic, and contextual) of needs of young children. This framework also serves as a lens that advocates diversity, equity, inclusion, inclusivity, and social justice in the context of education by viewing children's learning as intertwined within these four complex and interconnected perspectives that beckon respect and consideration. It also makes explicit that the teachers' teaching work needs to revolve around children and their unique characteristics and circumstances.

5 | The Four Cornerstones of Responsive Practice Framework

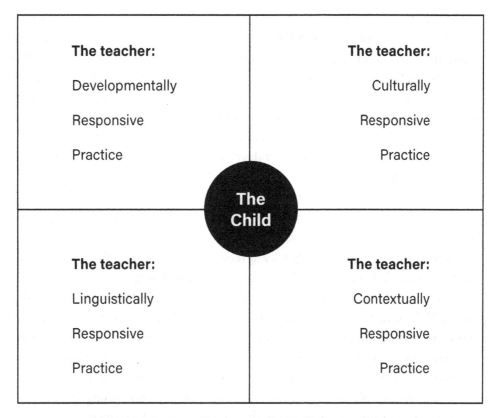

Figure 2. The Four Cornerstones of Responsive Practice: A Theoretical and Practical Framework.

Developmentally Responsive Practice

Developmentally responsive practice refers to teaching practices that consider children's individual and common developmental characteristics. It is widely established that early childhood is a critical period because the neurological connections formed during this time lay the foundation for later development in various areas (e.g., cognitive, language, socioemotional, physical). Given this importance, early childhood educators need to support young children's development responsively in all areas. But to do so, these educators need guidance. NAEYC's developmentally appropriate practice is a theoretical and practical framework that provides such explicit guidance (Chen and Battaglia 2023). Thus, developmentally appropriate practice has been espoused as the gold standard of professional knowledge, skills, and dispositions for early childhood educators to follow in the United States and beyond.

According to NAEYC (2022), developmentally appropriate practice is premised on decades of child development theory, research, and practice in early childhood education. The developmentally appropriate practice framework is grounded in the theoretical contributions of constructivists, notably Jean Piaget and Lev Vygotsky. Piaget and Vygotsky both contributed to our understanding of how individuals go about learning and constructing knowledge. However, there are fundamental differences between these two theorists' ideologies. For instance, Piaget (1963) asserted that development precedes learning, thus centering individual experience as key to learning. In contrast, Vygotsky (1978) conceptualized learning as a driver of development and asserted that learning through social interaction with others is critical to development. Despite their differences in viewpoint regarding whether learning leads to development or vice versa, both Piaget and Vygotsky agreed that learning and development are interrelated and that both should be supported accordingly.

While both Piaget's and Vygotsky's constructivist ideologies are influential in NAEYC's developmentally appropriate practice framework, Piaget's work is more prominently highlighted, casting young children as active learners and individual constructors of their own knowledge. This is not to say that teachers are not actively involved in the children's development and learning. In fact, teachers play a critical role in creating opportunities for children to engage in child-centered learning experiences. From this individual constructivism perspective, early childhood educators would need to create individualized learning experiences (e.g., hands-on exploration and play-based activities) to cater to young children's unique strengths, needs, interests, and abilities, while recognizing these children's specific stages of cognitive development.

The developmentally appropriate practice framework emphasizes three core considerations (NAEYC 2020, 2022):

1. Commonality
2. Individuality
3. Context

With respect to commonality, developmentally appropriate practice encompasses age appropriateness, focusing on what is appropriate for children within a common age (NAEYC 2020, 2022). In this context, teachers who understand the typical patterns of behaviors and growth associated with certain age groups can better plan and deliver the most appropriate learning experiences for young children at a given age.

With respect to individuality, developmentally appropriate practice emphasizes incorporating knowledge of each child's individual needs based on factors such as family backgrounds and personal characteristics (age, interests, abilities, strengths, support needs) (NAEYC 2020, 2022). Additionally, considering that children express their understanding and ideas in myriad ways, the developmentally appropriate practice framework advocates a variety of effective means to teach the same content so that these children's diverse individual learning and developmental needs are addressed. The idea of multiple approaches to teaching promotes diversity, equity, inclusion, inclusivity, and social justice and encourages educators to access and promote children's diverse means of understanding and interpretation. This idea is also supported by the metaphor of "a Hundred Languages" embraced and advocated by the Reggio Emilia approach (Edwards, Gandini, and Forman 2012).

Additionally, developmentally appropriate practice recognizes the significance of context (NAEYC 2020, 2022). For instance, educators consider the social, cultural, and linguistic contexts in which children are situated when making instructional decisions. By understanding these diverse contexts, early childhood educators can incorporate such knowledge in creating inclusive and meaningful environments and experiences to better support these children's learning and developmental needs.

Culturally Responsive Practice

Culturally responsive practice refers to teaching practices that consider the cultural backgrounds affecting individual children's development and learning. It urges educators to consider the children's "funds of knowledge" (Moll et al. 1992), including the richness of the cultural and linguistic assets that children bring to the classroom from home. Mari Riojas-Cortez (2001) found that bilingual programs benefited Mexican American preschool children who were encouraged and felt comfortable to apply cultural aspects of their funds of knowledge (language, values, beliefs) during sociodramatic play episodes. Furthermore, research has found that the ability to speak two languages can enhance children's social interactions and leadership skills. For example, in the study that I conducted with Crystal Kacerek on leadership and followership of twenty racial/ethnic minority preschool children (most of whom were Spanish speakers), we revealed some interesting findings (Chen and Kacerek 2022). Specifically, by having the ability to co-switch (or alternate) between Spanish and English in their conversations with Spanish-English bilingual speakers during sociodramatic play, the dominant leaders in the dramatic play groups were effective in leading both their English- and Spanish-speaking peers, especially those who were linguistically less advanced.

As student populations in classrooms throughout the United States become increasingly diverse and even superdiverse, it is essential that teachers develop and enhance their cultural competence. Cultural competence refers generally to the knowledge, skills, and attitudes required to effectively interact and communicate with others in a culturally diverse environment (Leighton and Harkins 2010). Engaging in culturally responsive practice means that teachers incorporate the diverse backgrounds, needs, and learning styles of children into their teaching practices (Phuntsog 2001). Additionally, it entails creating a respectful environment that acknowledges cultural differences without passing judgment on other cultures (Suh 2004). These findings also suggest that teachers who possess cultural competence are likely to become more attuned to and considerate of the learning needs of culturally and linguistically diverse learners.

The question is, *how can educators become culturally competent?*

Educators can become (more) culturally competent through professional learning and self-reflection. First, educators may operate from their own cultural assumptions, and thus teach based on what they know and believe about other cultures. In this case, educators need to recognize how their cultural heritage and assumptions can influence their attitudes and beliefs toward the backgrounds of the children they teach. Second, beyond this recognition, educators can benefit from gaining a clearer understanding of their own culture and that of others. They can do so by proactively conducting research and engaging in dialogue with others, learning about the cultural values, expectations, and attitudes held by their learners. This approach can form a strong foundation on which to build their understanding and connections with the children and their families. By "knowing thyself" and actively learning about the cultures of their students through continuous and intentional professional development, teachers can cultivate equity, inclusivity, as well as appreciation of and respect for cultural diversity within the classroom.

Additionally, it is crucial that teachers approach cultural diversity with respect and an open mind, recognizing that they may unconsciously hold biases or misconceptions about culturally and linguistically diverse learners, particularly DLLs, and their families. For example, a teacher notices that a recently arrived immigrant child from China avoids making direct eye contact when interacting with authority figures. Lacking the knowledge that this gesture is a typical sign of respect in Chinese culture, the teacher may misinterpret the child's action as disrespectful or believe that it is indicative of an underlying developmental issue.

However, an open-minded and culturally competent teacher would capitalize on this situation as an opportunity for learning. They could initiate conversations with the child's family or consult individuals from the same Chinese cultural background to gain insight into this specific behavior. This proactive approach can potentially dispel misinterpretations or biases and provide an opportunity for teachers to develop a more nuanced understanding of behaviors beyond their own cultural frame of reference.

Linguistically Responsive Practice

Linguistically responsive practice refers to teaching practices that consider the linguistic backgrounds affecting individual children's development and learning. All children, especially DLLs, can benefit from their teachers' linguistically responsive practice. Indeed, newcomers from other countries may experience emotional turmoil in an unfamiliar classroom where their native language is not understood or reinforced. There are many ways through which teachers can engage in linguistically responsive practice. For instance, a teacher may choose to communicate with DLLs in their home language. If teachers are not proficient in the DLLs' home language, they can learn some essential words and phrases in that language to facilitate communication with both the DLLs and their families.

When working with DLLs, teachers should respect these learners' home languages and cultures while helping them build the English proficiency and cultural knowledge they need to succeed in school and later in society. Furthermore, it is important that early childhood teachers help DLLs bridge two different languages and cultures and make a successful transition from home to school. In this process, teachers should pay close attention to the duration of and the circumstances surrounding the child's language learning in both their home language and English, the child's proficiency in each language, and language use in the home (as discussed in chapters 3 and 4).

Contextually Responsive Practice

Contextually responsive practice refers to teaching practices that consider the various contextual factors/characteristics affecting individual children's development and learning. NAEYC (2020) emphasized the importance of incorporating knowledge of the diverse contexts within which each child develops and learns in developmentally appropriate ways, and thus context is included as one of the three core considerations of the developmentally appropriate practice framework. A practice is only truly developmentally appropriate in nature if it considers contextual factors, including the child's cultural and linguistic assets as well as developmental abilities, strengths, and needs. The corollary is that a practice is *not* developmentally appropriate if it does not consider the various contexts in which a child is situated, socialized, lives, learns, develops, and grows. Thus, it is through a proper understanding of the child's contextual factors/characteristics that early childhood educators can effectively tailor their teaching approaches to meet the child's unique learning and developmental needs. It is also through a holistic consideration of contextual factors situating the child that early childhood educators can create a truly equitable, inclusive, and supportive learning environment that enables the child to thrive.

Chapter Conclusion

While the landscape of early childhood education in the United States is constantly changing, developmentally appropriate practice remains the constant as the gold standard for teaching young children. Incorporating the developmentally appropriate practice framework, I delineated the Four Cornerstones of Responsive Practice framework that beckons educators to first understand and then engage in developmentally, culturally, linguistically, and contextually responsive practice that is so critical to meeting the diverse learning needs of all children, especially DLLs. While each dimension is targeting specific concerns, the four dimensions of responsive practice should be treated as a collective and implemented holistically to better tailor to the learning strengths and needs of DLLs as whole learners. The preceding approaches reflecting each of the Four Cornerstones of Responsive Practice are demonstrated in the case narratives presented in chapters 6–8. These case narratives demonstrate that the Four Cornerstones of Responsive Practice are a sustainable framework to apply in working with learners from diverse backgrounds.

Reflection Questions

- How have you incorporated or how might you incorporate the various developmental, cultural, linguistic, and contextual characteristics of children, especially DLLs, in your teaching?

- How have you ensured or how might you ensure that your practices are responsive to the learning needs of diverse learners in your classroom?

Part II: Case Studies

CHAPTER 6

Providing Responsive Teacher Scaffolding

What a child can do today with assistance, she will be able to do by herself tomorrow.

—Lev S. Vygotsky, Soviet psychologist

It is well established that during early childhood, children experience rapid development in all areas (physical, cognitive, social, emotional) that sets the foundation for future development (Shonkoff and Phillips 2000; Weiland and Yoshikawa 2013). By implication, then, the early childhood setting is a critical place for young children to learn and develop. Furthermore, from a sociocultural perspective, as learning is a socially and culturally embedded activity (Vygotsky 1978), the social ecology of the early childhood classroom can offer many opportunities for children to learn through interactions with adults and peers. Such social learning serves as a vital building block for advancing children's development. Particularly through social interaction, children not only communicate using language but also acquire and convey cultural values associated with that language. Importantly, Vygotsky's sociocultural theory suggests that while children actively construct knowledge of the reality of the world in which they live and make meaning of it, their learning will occur most potently within their *zone of proximal development* (ZPD). In the context of children's learning and development, Vygotsky's idea of ZPD is defined as the difference between what a child can achieve independently (the actual level of development) and what the child can achieve potentially with assistance from more competent individuals (the potential level of development). The idea of ZPD is depicted in figure 3.

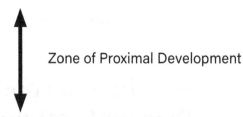

Figure 3. Vygotsky's zone of proximal development.

By the implication of ZPD, social partners (who can include teachers and more advanced peers) are in a unique position to bridge the children's learning through responsive scaffolding, which is defined as the assistance provided by more competent individuals to support those who are less advanced (Vygotsky 1978). The concept of *scaffolding* was first coined by David Wood and colleagues (1976, 90) to refer to a process whereby a tutor's assistance "enables a child or novice to solve a problem, carry out a task or achieve a goal which would be beyond his unassisted efforts." As children achieve their potential level of performance on a task, they will then establish a new ZPD. Thus, as the child's ZPD advances, a new goal needs to be set, and the target scaffolding is adjusted accordingly.

By assessing where a child's current and potential levels of development are, the teacher can then devise developmentally appropriate strategies. In the chapter "Understanding Learning and Tailoring Instruction" from my previous book (Chen 2016a), I delineated the importance of assessment, the different types of assessments, and examples of these assessments, all of which suggest that a comprehensive assessment system is needed to appropriately scaffold children's learning and development. When educators provide responsive scaffolding, they create a bridge between what the children know or can do and what they are capable of learning with assistance. For example, my collaborators and I have found in our research that teacher scaffolding benefits children's socioemotional learning (Chen and Adams 2022; Chen and Badolato 2023) and language development (Chen and Liang 2017). Teacher scaffolding can also help ease any frustration that the child may experience in completing a challenging task.

In the classroom ecology, the teacher is regarded as the authority who sets the tone for all social interactions and facilitates them among children. Social interactions usually require effective language skills, which can, in turn, contribute to learning and development. However, when children lack effective language skills, they may experience difficulties in other developmental areas. For instance, researchers have found that children with lower levels of language skills tend to demonstrate greater behavior problems and are more likely to experience peer rejections (Bichay-Awadalla et al. 2020). They also tend to be followers rather than leaders (Chen and Kacerek 2022).

Language skills are also foundational to children's later literacy development and academic success in formal schooling. Thus, educators should scaffold children's language acquisition, and there are ample opportunities for them to do so in the classroom. For instance, teachers can model appropriate oral language use and engage children in positive interactive conversations during classroom learning activities, whether they are child-initiated play/projects or teacher-guided/directed instruction. They can also use language-enhancing strategies such as asking questions, modeling language use, providing positive feedback, and engaging children in effective conflict resolution during peer interactions to scaffold children in using language effectively to develop prosocial behaviors. The teachers may also use specific strategies involving verbal communication and social skills to appropriately challenge the children's thinking and encourage their ability to problem solve. However, they should not provide mainly directives, such as commanding or telling children what to do. This strategy does not seem to facilitate children's language development or encourage them to engage in verbal interactions with adults as found in the research that I conducted with Sonja de Groot Kim (Chen and de Groot Kim 2014).

With respect to scaffolding the learning and development of culturally and linguistically diverse learners, teachers should design language and literacy-rich environments and experiences for these children, especially those who lack access to such resources at home, because the quality and quantity of rich language exchanges with adults are instrumental to children's language development (Chen and de Groot Kim 2014; Wasik and Hindman 2015). These opportunities encourage children to build requisite language skills and to practice them in social interactions with others in the classroom.

What follows are four case studies that demonstrate possibilities for responsive teacher scaffolding in action. They are analyzed using my proposed Four Cornerstones of Responsive Practice framework.

CASE STUDY #1:

Teacher Scaffolding of a Prekindergarten DLL's Acquisition of Language Skills and Engagement in Effective Social Interaction

Megan DiGuilio, prekindergarten teacher

Context

I teach a prekindergarten class at a private child care center in a suburban community. My class comprises fifteen children ages three to four. The majority (67 percent) of the children are White and the others are Hispanic (20 percent) and Indian (13 percent). Most of the parents of these children are from middle-class backgrounds and work full-time, leading them to rely heavily on the school to care for and educate their children. Most of the children attend the center on a tuition-based basis, and the rest of the children's tuition is covered by Catholic charities.

Although there are two other Hispanic children in the class, Vincent is the only Spanish-English DLL who speaks fluent Spanish and is only now learning English. He is the only child and the only grandchild in his family. Thus, he is lovingly doted on by both his parents as well as his grandfather who named him. Vincent's family speaks Spanish at home, but his mother can communicate with me and the school staff in English. This is Vincent's first year of preschool and his first time away from his family. School, along with its routines and rules, is something that Vincent is only now experiencing. Having no siblings or cousins, Vincent has never interacted with other children prior to attending school. The COVID-19 pandemic has further hindered his ability to find other children to socialize with.

Case Narrative

To help Vincent learn to listen and follow instructions, I rely on using my limited Spanish to interact with him. Vincent seems to appreciate the connection with me when I speak Spanish with him. However, this growing connection leads me to become the only teacher he will interact with. For instance, if my paraprofessional, another teacher, or an administrator were to try to communicate with him, he would not be able to focus on and engage in the interaction. Vincent also feels more comfortable engaging in independent activities within a learning center, as he can freely explore and play by himself without interacting with others. To encourage Vincent's development of social skills, I begin initiating interactions between him and other classmates within a learning center.

Today Vincent chooses to be in the dramatic play center as he has many times before. The dramatic play center is a favorite among the children because of its captivating toy kitchen play set. This particular area serves as a comforting haven for Vincent, as he is able to easily create his play theme with familiar words like *cocina* (kitchen), *comida* (food), and *cocinando* (cooking). There Vincent is joined by three other children, eagerly pretending to be chefs in a bustling pretend diner. Delving into a world of make-believe, the children are busy cooking noodles, scooping them into bowls, and speaking to one another about the number of place settings they need on the table. One child, Makayla, proudly places a wooden cake that she has decorated on the table. Vincent walks over to the cake, smiles, and then gets the play cake server and starts to pretend to slice up the cake. It is then that I hear Makayla's scream, "Miss Megan! Vincent! Vincent is breaking it! He is breaking my cake!" Vincent stands there confused and stunned. I realize that Vincent is at a loss for words. He knows he is unable to explain himself to her, recognizing that Makayla does not understand Spanish.

I need to step in to intervene. Makayla points and repeats again that Vincent was breaking her cake. I tell them both to take a deep breath, and I then encourage Makayla to allow Vincent to explain to her what his intentions were. Vincent very rapidly explains in Spanish what he was trying to do, while using hand gestures to try to get his point across. His Spanish is often a little hard to understand when he speaks too fast, and I often need to remind him to slow down and speak as clearly as he can. I tell him to take a deep breath and see if he can tell us in English. Vincent looks at Makayla, then at me, and back at Makayla again. I can tell from his eyes that he is frustrated, as he is trying to look for the right words to say: "I look. There done. I cut it." "Vincent, you noticed that the cake was ready, and you wanted to slice it and serve it to the customers," I confirmed with him, seeking clarity. Vincent nods affirmatively about his intent. Turning this communication challenge into a teachable moment, I take the opportunity to explain the importance of patience and understanding for both Vincent and Makayla to use their words to inquire and engage with their friends during pretend play. In doing so, I try to gently guide the children in fostering effective communication, empathy, and cooperation among them.

To further scaffold Vincent's learning in English, I make vocabulary and word pronunciation a main focus during academic activities. I also continue to observe his social interactions with his peers. In particular, I scaffold Vincent by modeling appropriate behaviors and words (e.g., "May I play with you?") that he can use to develop his pretend play skills and social interactions in a positive manner.

After a few weeks, I observe that Vincent's English ability has begun to improve little by little with my scaffolding. He has also gradually gained confidence and become more comfortable interacting with me and his peers in English.

Case Analysis Using the Four Cornerstones of Responsive Practice Framework

Developmentally Responsive Practice

While working with Vincent, Mrs. DiGuilio made concerted efforts to foster his social and emotional competence. Of particular importance among prekindergartners is their ability to navigate and negotiate their verbal interactions with others, which, in turn, can affect the other areas of their development. Keeping in mind Vincent's ZPD, Mrs. DiGuilio adopted developmentally responsive practice (such as modeling language use and social skills) to scaffold Vincent's acquisition of language and social skills to effectively interact with his peers. In doing so, Mrs. DiGuilio helped bridge Vincent's actual and potential levels of development. Furthermore, she also effectively fostered a caring and supportive learning community for the children in the classroom while creating the individualized learning experiences that Vincent needed to develop his English language skills and effective social interactions with others.

Culturally Responsive Practice

Mrs. DiGuilio applied several strategies to scaffold Vincent in developing English language skills and appropriate social interactions. Moving forward, she might also consider incorporating cultural activities that encourage Vincent to share his native culture and language with his peers, especially considering that he is the only DLL in the classroom. Furthermore, such cultural activities would be mutually beneficial to Vincent and his classmates in learning about one another's cultures and languages. In addition, this learning could encourage other children to become more understanding and compassionate toward Vincent's limitations in English language facility and social skills.

Linguistically Responsive Practice

Not having a common language to communicate with others can lead to misunderstandings. The communication challenge experienced by Vincent and Makayla highlights the need for children to foster mutual understanding in resolving conflicts. When Makayla misunderstood Vincent's intention and action, a conflict ensued. Mrs. DiGuilio seized this opportunity to transform the communication challenge into a teachable moment, gently guiding the two children by nurturing the values of effective communication, empathy, and cooperation. These essential skills are pivotal for navigating verbal interactions, problem solving, and conflict resolution among children, using means such as inquiring about one another's intentions and actions with words. Mrs. DiGuilio engaged in linguistically responsive practice with Vincent in several ways. For instance, she intentionally used her, albeit limited, Spanish to speak with Vincent when needed, through which she was able to create a special connection with him. To scaffold Vincent's acquisition of the English language and social skills, Mrs. DiGuilio continued to help him build vocabulary and guide him in word pronunciation, observe his linguistic interactions with peers, and model appropriate social behaviors and language use.

Contextually Responsive Practice

Mrs. DiGuilio considered several contextual factors when scaffolding Vincent in acquiring English as a second language and developing appropriate social skills. For instance, she observed that Vincent had limited interactions with other children due to the COVID-19 pandemic and that he was the only DLL in the classroom. Keeping this knowledge in mind, Mrs. DiGuilio made an intentional effort to observe Vincent's social interactions with his peers and model appropriate behaviors and words accordingly to help him develop prosocial and communication skills. For example, when Vincent and Makayla were having a conflict, Mrs. DiGuilio intervened and reminded them to use strategies such as asking questions and listening to what each other had to say about the situation.

CASE STUDY #2:

Teacher Scaffolding of a Preschool DLL's Acquisition of Language Skills Using a Variety of Strategies

Fatima Rafhan, Preschool Teacher

Context

I teach prekindergarten in a culturally and linguistically diverse school district. My class comprises fifteen children ages three to four. Among these children, 60 percent are Caucasians, 9 percent Latin Americans, 15 percent African Americans, and 16 percent Asians. I have previously taught DLLs. This school year I am working with Maxim, a four-year-old DLL who recently moved with his family to the United States from Ukraine. While Maxim and his parents speak only Ukrainian, his grandma has been living in the United States for the past twenty years and speaks both English and Ukrainian. In my school, English as a second language (ESL) services are not provided to children until kindergarten. Although the ESL teacher does visit my prekindergarten classroom twice a week to monitor the language growth of DLLs, the support is not sufficient for new DLLs who do not speak English. In addition, no adults or children in the school speak Ukrainian to connect with Maxim in this language.

Case Narrative

When the school year started in September, Maxim exhibited significant behavioral issues, causing disruptions to the other children in the classroom. I found myself pondering whether language was the sole reason for Maxim's behavioral difficulties or if there were other underlying issues.

One particular learning activity where Maxim struggled most was Buddy Reading time. He frequently became overwhelmed and confused when selecting a book to read. To support and motivate Maxim, I assembled some simple children's books written in Ukrainian and placed them in the Buddy Reading buckets for him to choose to read. Sure enough, the books in his familiar home language appeared to provide Maxim with a sense of comfort and motivation to read books.

During read-aloud activities, I employed scaffolding techniques to support Maxim's learning and understanding as well as promote his engagement. For instance, I encouraged him to show me how he should hold the book and turn the pages (which he already knew from reading children's books in Ukrainian) to actively involve him in using the same strategy when reading books in English. Moreover, to ensure that Maxim felt included and his home language valued, I displayed our daily schedule and other essential vocabulary (such as words from the books we read) in both English and Ukrainian, accompanied by visual aids. These visual accompaniments included a specifically tailored communication chart featuring essential expressions and associated pictures. This visual aid enabled and empowered Maxim to communicate his needs by pointing to the corresponding images until he could use words to express them in English. Initially, Maxim relied solely on pointing to the pictures, but as the school year progressed, he was able to gradually use some English words from the chart.

In addition, to enhance Maxim's language comprehension, I utilized the total physical response (TPR) technique [developed by James Asher in the 1960s]. I used this technique with all children in the classroom, but it was particularly beneficial to Maxim's learning. First, I used vocabulary words from our readings that I intended to teach explicitly. Next, I provided various ways for the children to understand the meanings of the vocabulary words, using props, body movements, and facial expressions. Subsequently, I encouraged them to use the same props and imitate the same body movement and facial expression to demonstrate their understanding of the meaning of a particular word while simultaneously saying this word aloud. I also repeated this same process for all the vocabulary words to reinforce the children's learning. Furthermore, I used the same method for reinforcing the understanding of daily classroom routines (such as unpacking and packing materials in their book bags and transitioning from one activity to another). Additionally, I incorporated games and simple songs into our classroom activities to create meaningful and relatable experiences for the children to practice and apply the target vocabulary learned.

To further support the children's learning and development, I provided individualized instruction to them. I sought to intentionally foster in Maxim a greater sense of comfort and belonging within the classroom environment by experimenting with a new approach that honored and respected his home language. This approach involved my researching the Ukrainian language and seeking assistance from Maxim's grandma to translate English words into Ukrainian. Subsequently, I created signs with key vocabulary to display throughout the classroom in both English and Ukrainian to encourage Maxim to better comprehend and acquire new words in English. Moreover, I continued to supply Maxim with additional children's picture books in Ukrainian. In the process, I was able to help create a comfortable and familiar reading experience for Maxim. I observed that, in turn, Maxim was better able to engage in reading and develop his language skills at his own pace. Additionally, this individualized approach was proven instrumental in nurturing Maxim's love for reading while simultaneously supporting his native language development.

Moreover, I learned to say some commonly used phrases to Maxim in Ukrainian, such as "hello is привіт (*pryvit*)," "good morning is доброго ранку (*dobroho ranku*)," and "Do you have to go to the bathroom? is Чи потрібно вам йти в туалет (*Chy potrebno vam yty v tualet*)." In doing so, I was able to gain Maxim's trust as he felt more comfortable and confident in reaching out to me for help. Furthermore, recognizing the importance of peer interactions for preschool children, when assigning class jobs, I selected roles that would encourage Maxim to interact with his peers, such as being a snack helper and lunch helper, so that he could develop his communication skills and social engagement.

Another effective strategy that I employed in supporting Maxim's learning was establishing a positive partnership with his family. Since Maxim's grandma was proficient in English, she served as the translator during our meetings. On Back-to-School Night, I posted a "Welcome" sign in English, Spanish, and Ukrainian on my classroom door to create an inclusive and respectful environment for all the children and their families. During my meeting with Maxim's family (his mom and grandma as the translator), I emphasized the value of bilingualism while encouraging them to recognize Maxim's development of English proficiency as necessary for academic success in the United States. To further assist Maxim's family and empower them to learn English, I provided information about ESL classes for adults offered by the public library in the community. I believe that by providing resources for Maxim's family to learn English, it could serve as an encouragement to Maxim in his effort to learn English.

The previously described strategies are just a few examples of my intentional efforts to help make Maxim feel comfortable learning in a new classroom environment. These strategies seem to have gradually eased Maxim into group learning activities, and I have subsequently witnessed that his behavior has begun to improve. Importantly, the integration of the Ukrainian language in the classroom achieves multiple purposes: (1) it validates the value of Maxim's cultural and linguistic background; (2) it supports him in bridging English and the Ukrainian language; and (3) it facilitates his understanding and acquisition of vocabulary in both languages. By respecting, embracing, and including the Ukrainian language in the classroom environment, I was able to create an inclusive and supportive space where Maxim felt valued and empowered in his learning and bilingual development.

Case Analysis Using the Four Cornerstones of Responsive Practice Framework

Developmentally Responsive Practice

Ms. Rafhan engaged in developmental responsiveness in several ways, including actively involving Maxim in reading activities, using visual aids, and applying the total physical response technique to help him acquire vocabulary in English. All of these activities were responsive to Maxim's developmental needs.

Culturally Responsive Practice

By learning to say some words in Ukrainian and incorporating Ukrainian translations for some English words posted in the classroom, Ms. Rafhan demonstrated validation and respect for Maxim's native language and culture. This approach made Maxim feel supported, respected, and comfortable in a new learning environment.

Linguistically Responsive Practice

Ms. Rafhan made concerted efforts to make Maxim feel that his native culture and language were valued. These efforts included posting a daily schedule in

Ukrainian and English, learning to speak some common phrases in Ukrainian, and seeking the assistance of Maxim's grandma as a translator of materials from English to Ukrainian for Maxim and during meetings with his family.

Contextually Responsive Practice

To scaffold Maxim's development of the English language and social skills, Ms. Rafhan intentionally created opportunities for him to interact with his peers by assigning him classroom jobs, such as being a snack helper and lunch helper. Understanding the importance of teacher-family partnerships in children's education, Ms. Rafhan proactively sought to establish a positive partnership with Maxim's family. For instance, during the Back-to-School Night, she posted a "Welcome" sign on her classroom door written in Ukrainian and other languages as represented by the children. This simple yet respectful welcome gesture could serve as Ms. Rafhan's invitation to a positive partnership with Maxim's family and other families.

CASE STUDY #3:

Teacher Scaffolding of Kindergarten Spanish-English Bilingual Children's Rhyming in Spanish and Positive Transfer of Language Skills

Imelda Stiles, Kindergarten English-Spanish Bilingual Teacher

Context

I was teaching a bilingual kindergarten class in a bustling urban community. The class comprised eighteen five-year-olds, most of whom were from low-income families. While most of the children were born in the United States, a few had just recently arrived in the country, further enriching our classroom with a greater diversity of cultures and experiences. The children shared a Hispanic heritage and Spanish as their native language.

Case Narrative

As a bilingual teacher in this kindergarten class, I taught every subject in Spanish. One of the main goals of the language curriculum was learning how to rhyme. So, after teaching the children the concept of rhyming, I would encourage them to practice rhyming by giving them a word (e.g., *gato*) to generate a list of rhyming words (e.g., *pato*). For example, I would say *"casa,"* and then pick different children to share a word that rhymes with it. They would provide rhyming words, such as *taza, masa, pasa*, and *raza*. When they ran out of words, I would assess their understanding by asking if the word *ratón* would rhyme with *casa*. When they said, "No," I would then continue asking if the word *grasa* would rhyme with *casa*, and the children said, "Sí!" This assessment helped me determine if they understood the concept of rhyming. We did this rhyming activity about three times a week.

Furthermore, we listened to famous children's rhyming songs in Spanish, and together we would find all the rhyming words and make a list of them. The children became really good at rhyming, to the point that they would provide me with rhyming words beyond our lessons. Witnessing the children's learning and genuine engagement in conveying their understanding of rhyming brought me immense joy and pride. I also felt a deep sense of fulfillment, knowing that we had not only achieved the objective of mastering rhyming but also had fostered a love in these young learners for language and creativity in connecting words.

In this bilingual program, it was required for an ESL teacher, Mrs. Anderson, to come into the classroom for one class period every day. Mrs. Anderson followed the same curriculum but taught it in English. One day Mrs. Anderson's lesson was about rhyming words, and I informed her that the children were good at it based on my own observations, so I was surprised to find that when she asked the class if *cat* and *bat* rhymed, my students said, "No." This unexpected response prompted Mrs. Anderson to ask more similar questions to test the children's understanding of rhyming, and unfortunately, the children continued to provide incorrect answers. Sensing confusion, I stepped in and reminded them of our previous lessons on rhyming words in Spanish. While I felt relieved when some of my students recalled learning the concept, I noticed that they still struggled to generate rhymes for certain words (e.g., *dog*) in English. I observed that this difficulty was likely due to their limited English vocabulary. Acknowledging this challenge and based on her evaluation, Mrs. Anderson concluded that the students were behind in their English language development and would require additional practice to catch up, especially in terms of rhyming in English. This assessment was also based on the recognition that expanding the children's English vocabulary would enhance their ability to comprehend and produce rhyming words in English.

Realizing the importance of helping the children transfer their understanding of rhyming words from Spanish to English, I implemented a strategy to support their development by incorporating two or three English words during our regular rhyming practice sessions even though my primary instruction was in Spanish. When some of the children expressed their unfamiliarity with the English words, I reassured them that understanding the meaning of the words was not necessary for this particular rhyming exercise. Instead, I encouraged them to listen to the ending sounds and determine whether they shared the same sound or not. By employing this strategy, I sought to facilitate positive transfer of rhyming skill in Spanish to their English instruction, even when encountering unfamiliar vocabulary.

My goal was not to focus on building their English vocabulary since I wasn't their ESL teacher, but to help them transfer the concept of rhyming from Spanish to English. Most of the children were able to do it, but they liked it more in Spanish since they had a bigger vocabulary in this language, and thus could come up with more words than they could in English. Nonetheless, I was delighted by their progress and was confident that they would get better at rhyming in both English and Spanish as they continued to build their vocabulary in both languages.

Case Analysis Using the Four Cornerstones of Responsive Practice Framework

Developmentally Responsive Practice

Ms. Stiles intentionally crafted a lesson and practice activities on rhyming in Spanish that aligned with the children's current stage of cognitive development. This responsiveness ensured that the lessons and related activities were both meaningful and appropriate in meeting the children's developmental and learning needs and in advancing their language competence in Spanish. The rhyming lessons and activities were also developmentally appropriate as they were part of the curriculum for these children's grade level—kindergarten.

Culturally Responsive Practice

Ms. Stiles incorporated rhyming songs in Spanish for her DLLs to listen to and search for rhyming words. Culturally relevant and familiar songs have a special way of drawing children's attention and inviting their engagement to reinforce their learning. Furthermore, by incorporating a cultural dimension into teaching rhyming, Ms. Stiles provided a valuable opportunity for her DLLs to make meaningful connections with their native culture and language. To build further connections, Ms. Stiles could continue leveraging culturally relevant rhymes, poems, or songs from the native countries of her Spanish-speaking DLLs. This approach would not only enhance their engagement and interest but also validate and honor their cultural identities. This inclusive approach would also foster a sense of belonging and create a supportive environment where DLLs could see themselves as reflected meaningfully in the learning materials and activities.

Linguistically Responsive Practice

Ms. Stiles recognized rhyming as a critical aspect of language learning within the kindergarten curriculum. Thus, she continued to facilitate and reinforce the children's understanding of rhyming in Spanish through lessons and further exercises. She also began to successfully facilitate the children's positive transfer of rhyming skills from Spanish to English through explicit instruction and practice.

Contextually Responsive Practice

Upon reflection, Ms. Stiles demonstrated contextual responsiveness by recognizing her DLLs' limited English proficiency as a likely hindrance to their understanding of rhyming in English. When reflecting on the confusion and difficulty the children experienced while generating rhyming words in English, Ms. Stiles addressed this particular challenge proactively. Specifically, she implemented a bilingual learning strategy that effectively leveraged and encouraged the positive transfer of cognitive skills of rhyming from Spanish to English. This strategic approach served as an effective scaffold to enhance DLLs' comprehension of rhyming in English while simultaneously strengthening their continued mastery of rhyming in Spanish. Another critical contextual factor in the children's successful bilingual development is the open communication that Ms. Stiles maintained with Mrs. Anderson so they could collaborate by exchanging assessment and observational insights, educational resources, and instructional strategies.

Through her responsive practice incorporating her knowledge of the contextual factors surrounding her DLLs' learning, Ms. Stiles promoted a sense of familiarity and confidence in her DLLs as they continued to learn English and Spanish simultaneously in a bilingual program. Ms. Stiles could introduce additional strategies that would encourage her DLLs to make connections between Spanish and English by ways such as explicitly drawing attention to the similarities and differences in rhyming between the two languages. This strategy could further encourage positive transfer of cognitive skills from Spanish to English to enhance the DLLs' bilingual development.

6 | Providing Responsive Teacher Scaffolding

CASE STUDY #4:

Teacher Scaffolding of DLLs' Academic Writing in Second Grade

ChareMone' Perez, Second Grade Teacher of English-Spanish DLLs

Context

I teach in a school district with a large student population of 8,000 students, mostly from low-income backgrounds, as indicated by 80 percent of them receiving free or reduced lunches. Most of the students there are minorities, with 75.5 percent being Hispanics and 42 percent English language learners (ELLs). Because of the large Hispanic population in my school, there is a bilingual program at each grade level. My school district requires students in second grade to be taught in a 50/50 model (50 percent in English and 50 percent in Spanish). As a second-grade teacher in this bilingual program, I teach reading, writing, math, social studies, and science in English, and my partner teacher teaches these same subjects in Spanish. We alternate teaching two homeroom classes for a three-week period. I teach a total of fifty-five students for the two classes, of whom twenty-eight students are from my homeroom class.

The students in each homeroom class receive a total of 160 minutes of literacy instruction daily. In my own homeroom class, the students are evaluated as performing in the literacy area either below or approaching the grade level according to the initial assessment results. The language assessment results also show that these students are not proficient in English or Spanish. Furthermore, even though these students may share the same language of Spanish, they have different cultures as they are from various Latin countries: 52 percent of the students in the class come from the Central American countries of Guatemala, Honduras, and El Salvador, and three students come from the South American country of Ecuador. Furthermore, my students have varying levels of education due to the interrupted or limited learning they received during the COVID-19 pandemic or due to their recent relocation to the United States.

Case Narrative

In working with DLLs in my second-grade class, I have observed that they frequently encounter difficulties, especially in grasping concepts, due to language barriers. The aspect that I perceive as particularly challenging for my students is completing writing assignments. Although these students have difficulty with writing, I have found that they are capable of accomplishing writing tasks when provided with an adequate level of scaffold that considers their emerging literacy skills.

At the start of the academic year, I administered an initial writing task to evaluate the students' writing abilities in English. This brief assignment required them to write about their favorite dessert and explain their reasons for liking it. Initially, the students exhibited great enthusiasm when I introduced the writing topic, and we even discussed it as a class. They were excited to share their ideas with their peers, and many were able to provide detailed explanations for why they enjoyed their favorite dessert. Subsequently, I provided the students with a writing template that included a picture box at the top and lines below for writing. Upon collecting their completed assignments, however, I noticed that nearly all the students simply drew a picture, while only some wrote a word or a few by using phonological skills that were below the level expected in second grade.

In a subsequent writing assignment in English and in accordance with my school district's writing curriculum, I tasked my students with writing a descriptive essay. The essay prompt required the students to describe their own unique imaginative monster and provide enough detail in their writing for their peers to correctly identify their monster drawing to be displayed on our class bulletin board. The monster theme appeared culturally meaningful as it was during the time of Halloween. Recognizing the writing abilities of my students, I understood that they would benefit from additional support to complete this assignment. Consequently, I approached this issue by providing scaffolded support to achieve what Vygotsky described as the zone of proximal development.

I implemented scaffolded writing support for my students by breaking down the assignment into manageable chunks. This approach involved providing clear, detailed instructions for each part of the writing task, including brainstorming, drafting, editing, revising, and publishing. As writing is a process, the entire assignment spanned over a period of three weeks. To begin, I taught the students about what adjectives are and their role as a part of speech, which was an integral aspect of this descriptive assignment. Throughout the duration of the writing task, I scaffolded the students' writing by incorporating various mini assignments for both classwork and homework that focused on identifying adjectives. Furthermore, to support my students with this writing task, I conducted conferences with each student at various stages of the writing process to ensure that they met the expectations while considering their individual skill levels. As emergent writers, many of my students were transitioning from relying on drawings to expressing their ideas in a few written words. To scaffold the students further, I provided sentence frames when necessary and created a word bank accompanied by corresponding pictures to support their understanding of new vocabulary. The word bank proved to be instrumental as it offered visual representations of words that could be used to describe their individual monster. For instance, I would write the word *slimy* and include a picture of a snail with a trail of slime to help the students build vocabulary and understanding of the meaning of this new adjective learned.

I also offered scaffolded support in Spanish, allowing students to write in Spanish and assisting them in translating their writing during the editing and revising phases of the writing process. When editing their writing pieces, I allowed students to use online tools such as Google Translate and online dictionaries. Additionally, I provided opportunities for peer editing.

Upon reflection, I have come to realize that my students encountered various challenges with initiating and completing writing tasks in English. However, I have found that the most effective approach to helping them overcome their writing barriers is by offering scaffolded support. For example, I provided individualized learning experiences catering to the students' specific needs and offering appropriate targeted assistance and feedback. As a result, I have noticed that the students have made gradual progress in their writing skills as they were able to apply what they have learned in subsequent writing assignments.

Case Analysis Using the Four Cornerstones of Responsive Practice Framework

Developmentally Responsive Practice

When Ms. Perez noticed that the DLLs in her second-grade homeroom class were performing either below or approaching grade level in reading and writing and that they were having difficulties with academic writing, she decided to scaffold their learning by achieving what Vygotsky described as the zone of proximal development (that is, bridging her students' actual and potential levels of development) in producing academic writing with expressive language skills in English. Academic writing, as an aspect of cognitive academic language proficiency (CALP; as discussed in chapter 4), is necessary and developmentally appropriate for students to acquire to succeed in school. To scaffold her students with an academic writing piece, Ms. Perez divided the writing assignment into smaller and more manageable tasks for them to accomplish over a period of time. Furthermore, to scaffold the DLLs in writing a successful descriptive essay about a monster in English, Ms. Perez taught the DLLs how to use adjectives. She also incorporated various mini-assignments to build up the DLLs' skills. Additionally, after conferencing with her students to learn about their learning strengths and needs, Ms. Perez began providing individualized support to meet each DLL's specific learning needs accordingly.

Culturally Responsive Practice

Ms. Perez demonstrated culturally responsive practice by allowing her students to integrate their native language of Spanish in writing a creative descriptive essay about their own monster. This writing topic was considered appropriate during Halloween—a culturally familiar holiday in the United States. Ms. Perez might also consider scaffolding her students by having them write a descriptive essay on a topic that is more relevant to their native culture, such as a holiday or tradition that they celebrated in their home country or still celebrate in the United States.

Linguistically Responsive Practice

Many of Ms. Perez's students experienced difficulties in initiating and completing writing tasks in English. Recognizing the writing abilities of her students and noticing that language barriers were a hurdle, Ms. Perez offered scaffolded support by providing explicit instruction on what adjectives are and how to use them in descriptive essays. She also encouraged her students to complete their descriptive essays about a monster in Spanish in the initial draft to help them apply their expressive language skills by articulating their ideas in writing. She then asked them to translate their written essays from Spanish to English during the editing and revising phases of the writing process. Additionally, Ms. Perez allowed her DLLs to leverage online tools such as Google Translate and dictionaries. Furthermore, she provided opportunities for peer editing. All of these opportunities served as valuable scaffolds for the students to meet their language needs.

Contextually Responsive Practice

In reflecting on the challenges of working with her second-grade English-Spanish bilingual class, Ms. Perez intentionally considered the context in which her students were situated. For example, she understood that many of her students were from low-income backgrounds and were not fully proficient in English nor Spanish. Additionally, many of her students' prior schooling was limited as a result of the COVID-19 pandemic and/or their recent relocation to the United States. Ms. Perez noticed that due to these various challenges, many of her students struggled with learning English, especially in academic writing. Accordingly, she demonstrated contextually responsive practice by providing scaffolded support, especially explicit instruction and individualized feedback to meet her students' specific learning needs.

The Acquisition of Language Skills in DLLs: Implications for Teaching

The various types of critical language skills, notably receptive and expressive language as embedded in BICS and CALP, have important implications for teaching practice. For example, to scaffold receptive and expressive language development in DLLs, early childhood educators can use supportive instructional strategies, including providing ample opportunities for children to engage in social interactions and conversations with one another, as was the case in Mrs. DiGuilio's teaching.

As BICS and CALP encompass different skill sets, they also require different strategies (as discussed in chapter 4). For instance, while the acquisition of BICS requires exposure and practice through social interactions in informal settings, acquiring CALP requires time and explicit language instruction. For example, teachers can explicitly teach academic vocabulary to DLLs by providing time for these children to incorporate the newly acquired vocabulary in academic discussion, presentation, and writing, as well as modeling the use of academic language, as was the case in Ms. Perez's teaching of academic writing. Furthermore, it is possible that a DLL may understand a concept but may not have mastered the academic language to express their understanding in English. It is also possible that a DLL may understand or be able to explain the concept in their home language but not in English. In this case, the teacher can find ways to help the DLL transfer the cognitive skills from their home language to English, especially if there exists common underlying proficiency (CUP) between the two languages (as discussed in chapter 4). This strategy was evident in Ms. Stiles's teaching of rhyming words.

To communicate effectively with others in informal social interactions, all children need to develop BICS, which are foundational skills involving the use of everyday, context-dependent language. To better scaffold DLLs' development of BICS, it is crucial that teachers provide "comprehensible input" that is understandable to DLLs, enabling them to grasp the content being taught or communicated through context clues or other modes, such as visual accompaniments and nonverbal cues (Krashen 1985). This strategy was demonstrated by Ms. Rafhan in scaffolding a DLL in learning English as a second language.

When DLLs begin learning their second language, it is developmentally appropriate for them to engage in what Krashen (1985) called the "silent period" or the "pre-production" stage. During this period, the child exhibits reluctance to verbally communicate in this new language but is acquiring receptive vocabulary (understanding what they hear) by listening to others speak and interact. This silent phase is transient, as the child may begin to speak within a few days to a year, depending on their personality and socialization experiences. During this process, it is important that the teacher respects DLLs by providing them the time and space to process and patiently wait for them to speak when ready rather than pressuring them to do so, as this approach can be counterproductive.

DLLs may also progress through what Tabors and Snow (1994) described as the four stages of second language acquisition:

1. **Home Language Use:** using mainly one's home language to communicate
2. **Nonverbal Period:** using nonverbal cues (including facial expressions, visuals, gestures, and body language) rather than language to communicate
3. **Telegraphic and Formulaic Speech:** using short and simple phrases (rather than sentences) consisting of mainly nouns and verbs, such as "Me eat" instead of "I am eating"
4. **Productive Language:** producing spoken and written language

To determine a DLL's stage of second language acquisition to provide proper scaffolding accordingly, it is important that the teacher devotes efforts to assess the child's language learning through formal and informal assessments (such as language screening tests and observations, respectively). That way the teacher will be better able to support the DLL's development of BICS as well as CALP according to their stage of second language acquisition. In a bilingual or dual language program, DLLs receive language learning and support in two languages, and thus their bilingual development is likely to be well supported. However, in a monolingual classroom, the teacher (especially one who does not speak the DLLs' native language) will need to find ways to incorporate children's culture and language in the teaching-learning process to show respect and inclusivity as they help DLLs acquire a second language or transfer cognitive and language skills from their first language to this second language.

CALP is particularly challenging for many children (as discussed in chapter 4), especially for DLLs, as demonstrated by the four case studies in this chapter. Yet CALP is critical for success in school and other academic settings. Thus, in addition to the teacher strategies described in the four case studies, I provide the following strategies that educators might consider revisiting or adding to their teaching toolboxes for use when supporting DLLs' development of CALP:

1. **Teacher modeling.** The teacher can model academic language use. For example, the teacher can model how to articulate one's viewpoint by saying, "I believe that the main character in the story is kind because . . . ."
2. **Providing scaffolding.** The teacher can apply known academic words to help DLLs understand new and more complex vocabulary. For instance, the teacher can explain the new word *delighted* to DLLs by using vocabulary that they already know, like its synonym *happy*.
3. **Assessing what DLLs already know in their home language.** Through assessment, the teacher can then leverage knowledge of the DLLs' linguistic and cultural backgrounds to help them acquire academic language proficiency in English. For example, the teacher can help a Chinese DLL understand the word *celebration* by asking her to describe an important holiday that she enjoyed in her home country.
4. **Communicating and teaching academic content.** The teacher can leverage visual aids, such as physical models and graphic organizers. For instance, the teacher can use a physical model to teach the children different parts of the body or compare two characters in the story by introducing the concepts of similarities and differences using a Venn diagram.
5. **Engaging in academic discussion.** The teacher can engage children in book discussions through which DLLs can learn from the teacher and other children how to use academic language. For example, the teacher can ask a linguistically more advanced child, "What is your opinion of the main character?" When the child responds by saying, "My opinion of the main character is that . . ." DLLs can learn to respond using a similar academic language structure when the teacher asks them the same question.
6. **Remembering and reinforcing learning of new vocabulary.** The teacher can help DLLs develop strategies for remembering newly learned words. For instance, the teacher can make a word wall of new words and write a sentence containing the newly added word. The teacher can also create a word bank in a notebook and encourage DLLs to create their own to help them remember the new words they have learned.
7. **Pairing or grouping DLLs with linguistically more advanced peers.** The teacher can pair or group DLLs with linguistically more competent peers in decontextualized activities, such as role plays, debates, plays, and skits. For example, the teacher can orchestrate a play

for DLLs to learn from their peers new academic words and language structures.
8. **Providing opportunities to engage DLLs in different forms of writing.** The teacher can teach or model the social etiquette and pragmatics of language use. For instance, the teacher can teach DLLs how to address different people in a formal letter or introduce the conventions of writing creative stories and poems.

Chapter Conclusion

As acquiring language skills is a complex and dynamic process that requires time, exposure, and practice, teachers are in a unique position to scaffold children's language learning and development of receptive and expressive skills, especially in BICS and CALP, by using strategies such as direct teaching, modeling, providing a language- and literacy-rich environment, engaging children in language- and literacy-promoting activities, and affording ample opportunities for practice. More importantly, as illustrated through the case narratives, teacher scaffolding is key. The cases presented by early childhood teachers in this chapter offer many examples of how they understood and utilized multiple scaffolding strategies to support DLLs' learning that aligned with the Four Cornerstones of Responsive Practice framework. These teachers' firsthand accounts demonstrate intentionality in their teaching practices. They reinforce the idea that developmentally, culturally, linguistically, and contextually appropriate strategies involve respecting and leveraging DLLs' cultural and linguistic backgrounds as assets when supporting their developmental and contextual learning needs.

Reflection Questions

▎ What are some of the scaffolding strategies you have implemented or might consider implementing to support effective social interaction and language development in children, especially DLLs? Specifically, what strategies have you used or are considering using to promote the development of receptive skills, expressive skills, BICS, and CALP in children, especially DLLs?

▎ What specific areas of DLLs' learning and development have you successfully scaffolded or might you scaffold? Why, and how?

CHAPTER 7

Building Strong Teacher-Family and Teacher-Teacher Partnerships

No school can work well for children if parents and teachers do not act in partnership on behalf of the children's best interests.

—Dorothy H. Cohen, teacher and writer

This quote by Dorothy H. Cohen underscores the powerful impact of teacher-family partnerships on the education of children. The imperative for fostering these partnerships reflects and reinforces Urie Bronfenbrenner's (1979) socio-ecological theory, which asserts that the child develops within a concentric nest of interconnected contexts, spanning from the innermost microsystems (the family at home, the teachers and peers at school) to the mesosystems (the link between two microsystems, such as the connection between home and school), and finally to the outermost macrosystems (culture, society). According to this theory, by virtue of having the most immediate and direct contact with a child, parents and teachers exert the strongest influence on this child's development. Recognizing that family extends beyond the child's parents to include other members, such as siblings and grandparents, henceforth, I use the term "family" instead of "parents," unless "parent" or "parents" are specifically mentioned by the teachers in this book.

Parents are widely regarded as the child's first teachers. Thus, they hold a central role as the primary and most influential agents in socializing the child within a culture (Chen 2019). However, the cultural value and belief system into which a child is socialized may differ from that of the teacher or the school. This is another good reason for fostering strong, positive partnerships between teachers and families to promote effective communication, cultural respect, and a shared understanding of each other's educational expectations for the child. Thus, engaging positively with families should not be seen as an add-on chore, but as a necessary and natural aspect of what teachers must do to further facilitate student learning and development.

A strong mesosystem is forged when the two microsystems of the home and the school are connected and trusting professional relationships between the teacher and different families are built, with the child's best interests at heart (see figure 4).

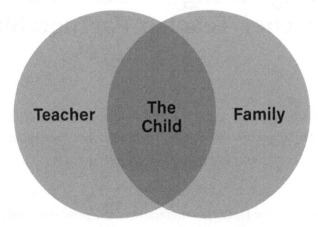

Figure 4. The child is shown as the shared responsibility of the teacher and the family in the educational process.

Given that the child is the shared responsibility of the teacher and the family, it is not surprising that a positive teacher-family partnership in the child's educational process is endorsed by NAEYC (2019) as a critical feature of its accreditation standards and educators' developmentally appropriate practice. Specifically, as advocated by NAEYC (2020, 14), a key element of developmentally appropriate practice involves "engaging in reciprocal partnerships with families and fostering community connections."

As the two most critical, immediate stakeholders in the child's education, both the teacher and the family must be willing to establish a strong, positive partnership in this educational process. However, the teacher-family partnership is not necessarily a straightforward process, but a dynamic, complex one that is influenced by a variety of factors. These factors encompass the teachers' ability to effectively communicate with families from culturally and linguistically diverse backgrounds, as well as the perceptions held by both teachers and parents regarding their respective roles (Chen 2016a). As in some cultures, teachers are highly respected as authority figures in the children's education, and thus they should be the first to initiate the communication channel and continue to engage in communication with families. Moreover, due to a lack of familiarity with the education system in the United States, those DLLs' parents from other countries and cultures may not understand what their role is within this new system and how to appropriately get involved in their children's education. For these two reasons alone, teachers are better positioned to promote family engagement and foster strong partnerships with DLLs' families through effective communication.

Effective Communication with Families

Effective communication with families can take a variety of forms, including oral and written, as well as unidirectional/one-way and bidirectional/two-way communication (Chen 2016a). Unidirectional communication includes methods such as the teacher sharing curriculum information with parents during face-to-face meetings or back-to-school nights, on a website, or in class newsletters or notes (Chen 2016a). Bidirectional communication, such as face-to-face conferences or meetings and phone calls between the teacher and the family, may be particularly effective in fostering mutual understanding about the child's developmental progress, strengths, behavioral and academic needs, as well as cultural and linguistic background and other characteristics (Chen 2016a). For instance, to establish mutual understanding, the teacher can invite the family to discuss each other's evaluation of the child's educational progress.

In this digital world, in addition to or in lieu of traditional face-to-face conferences, parents and teachers can communicate via email, virtual meetings, or other virtual platforms. When used effectively, digital technological tools can enhance teacher-family communication and connection. There are freely available digital tools that teachers can leverage to keep parents informed about a variety of matters, such as the students' learning progress, classroom and school happenings, events, and policies. For instance, the ClassDojo app has become a popular communication platform. According to ClassDojo's website (www.classdojo.com), some of its communication features include a feed for sharing materials, such as photos and videos from the school day and from home; instructional materials; and messages between teachers and families, which can be translated into many different languages. This translation capacity is particularly welcoming to families of DLLs.

Despite the pervasive usage and the purported benefits of digital tools, a reliance on these tools for communication may inadvertently create a false sense of teacher-family partnerships. Furthermore, it is also important to recognize that not all families are well versed with or actively leverage these digital tools to make good use of them, as revealed by the study that I conducted with Dahana Rivera-Vernazza (Chen and Rivera-Vernazza 2022). Another drawback is that while communication via these digital communication tools can facilitate immediate responses between teachers and families, it can be time-consuming and lead to information overload. Moreover, written messages exchanged through these digital platforms also can be prone to misinterpretation, resulting in misunderstandings of the intent and tone of the message. In such cases, the teacher and families should also consider meeting in person.

When the family does not know English, it is important that the teacher provides accurate translations of all communications in their home language. This approach not only promotes effective communication and positive teacher-family partnerships but also demonstrates respect for the families' diverse cultural and linguistic backgrounds. In cases where parents are illiterate in their home language, it becomes necessary to conduct communication orally, either in person or via the phone. In a superdiverse classroom, even if the teachers are multilingual, it may not be possible that they understand all the home languages represented in the classroom. Thus, in cases where the teacher does not speak the home language of the children's families, it is important that a translator/interpreter is made available. Recognizing that communication plays a vital role in fostering strong teacher-family partnerships, teachers should make concerted efforts to seek additional resources and collaborate with their fellow teachers to share experiences and strategies for effectively engaging with families from culturally and linguistically diverse backgrounds.

Any effective approach to communicating with families, regardless of the method or platform used, must be conducted in a respectful manner. Here are some approaches teachers can apply to foster effective and respectful communication with families:

- **The "sandwich" approach:** This approach is particularly effective if you have concerns about the child. In my previous book (Chen, 2016a), I described this approach as follows: "The direction of the conversation goes from positive to negative and back to positive, sandwiching the negative between two positive statements. Specifically, you state some positive things about the child in the beginning, gradually ease into the middle of the conversation when you raise concerns and provide evidence, and finally conclude with a positive outlook by offering suggestions, encouragements, and support" (85).

7 | Building Strong Teacher-Family and Teacher-Teacher Partnerships

- **The "seeking to understand and then be understood" approach** (Chen, 2016a): This approach entails listening respectfully to what the family has to say first before sharing your perspective on a particular matter related to the child during events such as teacher-family conferences. If their viewpoints or expectations differ from yours, it is especially important that you acknowledge, respect, and try to understand them. You can then strive to find common ground, keeping the child's best interest at heart.
- **The inclusive approach:** This approach involves demonstrating that you view the family as a vital partner in the child's educational process. This goal can be achieved by inviting the family to engage in bidirectional communication, participate in classroom activities (such as sharing about their cultures), and contribute to decision-making. Through mutual communication, both the educator and the family can exchange information about the child's learning and developmental progress to keep each other informed to better serve the child's learning needs.

As educational authorities, teachers are in a unique position to initiate communication channels, cultivate strong teacher-family partnerships, and seek to sustain these respectful partnerships throughout the child's education with them. Establishing and sustaining positive teacher-parent partnerships require intentionality, respect, and commitment on the part of the teacher. Given the complexities embedded in the superdiversity between and within culturally and linguistically diverse learners in the education system, effective partnerships between teachers and parents are more critical than ever to meet the developmental and learning needs of the children whom they both care about. By actively engaging with families, teachers can develop a deeper appreciation for the diverse perspectives and behaviors of their DLLs and take responsive actions to create an inclusive, respectful, and supportive learning environment for these children to thrive.

What follows are four case studies that demonstrate possibilities for creating strong teacher-parent and even teacher-teacher partnerships. They are analyzed using the Four Cornerstones of Responsive Practice framework.

CASE STUDY #1:

Connecting with an Infant by Connecting with the Family First
Josephine Ahmadein, Infant/Toddler Spanish-English Bilingual Educator

Context

In my role as head teacher of a NAEYC-accredited center for over thirty years, I have met numerous families from diverse cultural backgrounds who have given me the opportunity to embrace and empower them in our common quest to provide high-quality learning experiences for their children. Being multilingual myself, born in Spain, with culturally unique values and beliefs, I recognized early on the transformational need for connection, the authentic similarities that bind us, as families and providers, and the individual differences that teach us all.

My infant program served children from three to about eighteen months. The families often wondered about our abilities to support infants linguistically as well as educationally in our interactions and activities throughout the day. It was always reassuring when families appreciated how we included sign language and the children's home languages in our curriculum and teaching.

The gradual process of getting to know the teachers, other children, routines, and changes when beginning group care is an emotional one. It is not just a major adjustment and transition for the new children, but for staff and parents as well. Sharing hopes and concerns as well as goals and needs lays the groundwork for establishing positive relationships that will directly affect the developmental progress of very young children. This process never took on a stronger meaning until a few years ago, when I started caring for and educating Jerry, a five-month-old boy. Jerry's parents, both of Chinese descent, had just relocated from Barcelona, Spain, to the United States.

After an initial welcome phone call that I made to Jerry's parents, we scheduled our introductory meeting at the center to get to know each other, and most importantly, hear all about Jerry's strengths and needs. As I began to gather information, I learned that Jerry's mom, Gloria, was born in Spain and spoke fluent European Spanish. I remember our mutual expression of surprise at discovering that we both came from the same city. Gloria shared how much she missed the family she left behind in Barcelona and felt so fortunate to have Jerry in an environment where he could hear the maternal home language on a regular basis. Jerry was spoken to in Chinese at home by his dad, but his mom wanted to try to keep Spanish very present in Jerry's life.

7 | Building Strong Teacher-Family and Teacher-Teacher Partnerships

By the end of our first meeting, an instant connection had been formed. The meeting that briefly started in English turned into my first opportunity to establish a common bond by speaking in Spanish from then on. Gloria requested that I speak only in Spanish to Jerry during daily routines and activities. Understanding how important it was for Jerry to develop and maintain one of his home languages, namely, Spanish, I committed to supporting her.

Case Narrative

During our staff meeting, I shared about Jerry and his family's request that I interact with him in Spanish, and we began intentionally preparing the environment and making changes in materials and print that would enable us to accommodate this need in the most practical and efficient way. We started adding books, signs, posters, and labels of short phrases in Spanish that served as continuous reminders to keep me focused on speaking in Spanish. I translated many of the most popular lullabies and fingerplays to add to our transition times and floor experiences. While I often repeated what I said in Spanish and also in English when I was talking to other children, I made sure I only used Spanish with Jerry.

My daily reports communicated to Gloria included all the special activities and strategies used to encourage Jerry's receptive and productive language in Spanish at the center so Gloria could continue using them at home. Over a few months, Jerry began to speak some words. I recall *agua* (water) being his very first word. He loved water play, and it was a regular activity both indoors and outdoors. Jerry also loved books, and by his first birthday, he could often be seen and heard in the cozy area reading *avión* (plane) and *coche* (car). The more I labeled as well as read and sang to him during our daily one-on-one interactions, I started to notice that other infants were repeating the Spanish words Jerry used. I noticed this language behavior especially at mealtimes, when Jerry would ask for *más cookies* or *más agua* and the others would repeat it. It was like hearing his echo but from his friends. They were learning Spanish too.

My initial purpose of supporting one family's home language had not only been part of our curriculum, but it had also turned into a connecting tool for developing a strong, positive partnership with Jerry's family. It gave us fuel to continue to make our daily routines and activities with Jerry and children more intentional and focused.

Case Analysis Using the Four Cornerstones of Responsive Practice Framework

Developmentally Responsive Practice

From a developmental perspective, it is clear that children thrive on and learn through nurturing social interactions as positive language input facilitates and promotes language learning. For Jerry, the positive social interactions provided by Ms. Ahmadein proved particularly instrumental to his learning. Recognizing that children need high-quality language input to develop language and social skills, Ms. Ahmadein spoke solely Spanish with Jerry to facilitate his Spanish development. During their interactions, Ms. Ahmadein displayed genuine interest and active engagement, demonstrating her full attention and intentional commitment to nurturing Jerry's development as a capable individual and learner.

Culturally Responsive Practice

By scaffolding Jerry's language development in Spanish, Ms. Ahmadein intentionally sought to facilitate Jerry's understanding of an important aspect of his culture, namely, the uniqueness of his home language. Singing culturally meaningful songs in Spanish to Jerry also exposed him to cultural learning. Furthermore, coming from the same culture and language as Jerry's mom, Ms. Ahmadein was in the best position to create learning activities that supported Jerry's exploration of Spanish and its associated culture, especially through her own native cultural experience.

Linguistically Responsive Practice

Honoring Jerry's mother's request, Ms. Ahmadein made sure that she used only Spanish during her interactions with Jerry. Additionally, Ms. Ahmadein intentionally immersed Jerry in a Spanish language-rich environment, using materials (such as books, signs, posters, and labels) and singing to him in Spanish to develop his receptive language skills. These intentional strategies not only honored Jerry's linguistic background in Spanish but also provided him with ample opportunities for language exposure and engagement.

Contextually Responsive Practice

Ms. Ahmadein considered various contextual factors influencing Jerry's learning and development. For instance, Ms. Ahmadein capitalized on their shared cultural and language heritage as a contextual strength to effectively create a strong and positive connection with Jerry's mom. By speaking exclusively in Spanish with Jerry during their interactions as requested by his mom, Ms. Ahmadein demonstrated respect for the parent's wish. Recognizing the importance of effective communication with the family, Ms. Ahmadein also provided Jerry's mom with daily updates, sharing insights into his activities and her strategies for scaffolding his receptive and expressive language development in Spanish. All of Ms. Ahmadein's intentional efforts seemingly gained the trust of Jerry's mom and strengthened their connection, laying a solid foundation for a mutually respectful teacher-family partnership.

CASE STUDY #2:

Forming Positive Connections with a Preschool DLL and Her Family
Alexandra Diaz, Preschool Teacher

Context

During this particular school year amid COVID-19, I taught seven children in person in a preschool classroom in a large, linguistically and culturally diverse school district serving children from mostly low-income backgrounds. According to the community's sociodemographic data, the majority (76 percent) of residents primarily speak a language other than English, with Spanish being the most prevalent, followed by Creole and Portuguese. While the primary language of instruction is English, to serve the needs of the large Spanish-speaking population within the school district, the preschool program is required to have at least one Spanish-speaking teacher in the classroom. In my classroom, we have the advantage of both my teacher assistant and me being fluent in Spanish.

Case Narrative

Anna recently arrived from Brazil and speaks only Portuguese fluently. Although my teacher assistant and I are fluent in Spanish, it is challenging for us to understand what she is saying due to the differences between Spanish and Portuguese. We try hard to decipher certain words, but we still cannot understand the majority of her utterances. Google Translate is not always reliable, seemingly recognizing only Portuguese from Portugal and not the dialect from Brazil. Needless to say, the adjustment for Anna into this US school was not easy.

At the beginning of the school year, everything was foreign to Anna, and she was experiencing a challenging time adjusting. For one, due to her ability to speak only Portuguese, she was having a difficult time understanding others and being understood. For another, it was also her first extended separation from her mom, making her adjustment to this school setting even harder. Every day for nearly three weeks, Anna would cry incessantly, seemingly inconsolable. All she wanted was to be with her mom, as she repeatedly uttered, *"Eu quero minha mãe"* (I want my mother). During group and individual activities, she continued to cry and did not want to participate, prompting the other children to withdraw from engaging with her. Although there were a few moments when she ceased crying and engaged in play for a while, it proved to be short-lived. We attempted to communicate with her through Google Translate, but it often yielded erroneous translations. We also discovered that Anna's mom relied heavily on Google Translate and similarly produced inaccurate translations, which resulted in significant difficulty in our understanding of each other.

My teacher assistant and I gradually learned some basic words in Portuguese online to communicate with Anna and her mom, a strategy that had helped facilitate Anna's inclusion in group discussions. To further foster her engagement, we bought books in Portuguese for Anna to read and incorporated some culturally familiar songs during our music time. The other children also learned to say *obrigada* (thank you) in Portuguese to Anna to encourage her participation and show their appreciation. Additionally, we provided individualized attention by engaging her in solving puzzles and playing games to help her learn English. Slowly but surely, Anna began to stop crying and become more settled into the classroom routines with other children.

Over a period of a few weeks, we had witnessed Anna making consistent socioemotional and communicative progress. Although there were still language barriers, Anna was slowly starting to build confidence in herself to speak what she learned in English, participate in classroom activities, and play with her classmates. By incorporating elements of Anna's home culture and language within the classroom, we had also witnessed a significant improvement in her trust and confidence. For instance, Anna's face lit up when she heard us speak the few words in Portuguese that we had learned, and her curiosity piqued upon hearing Brazilian cultural songs. Furthermore, we took the time to understand Anna's interests and integrate them into classroom discussions and activities, thereby fostering a sense of inclusivity. For example, knowing that Anna enjoyed looking at the pictures in the children's book during story time, we allowed time for her to read the books in Portuguese with English translations to all of the children. This intentional act benefited Anna's learning as well as her relationship with the other children in the classroom. In turn, the children got to know Anna better and sought to involve Anna in their play.

Reflection and Conclusion

Upon reflection, I have concluded that the journey of working with Anna remains a work in progress. While we strive to learn Brazilian-style Portuguese, we are also trying to teach Anna English to facilitate her communication and comprehension skills in this language, as it is the medium of instruction in our classroom. Nonetheless, we will continue to make concerted efforts to create a culturally and linguistically inclusive and respectful environment where Anna feels comfortable, supported, and confident to thrive academically and socially.

As we navigate this teaching-learning process with Anna and her family, in addition to providing individualized instruction to Anna, we remain committed to representing her native culture and language through culturally meaningful books and songs. In doing so, we seek to cultivate a supportive and trusting relationship with Anna and her family. As she continues to adapt to living in a new country and learning in a new classroom environment, we are dedicated to helping her gradually overcome the language barriers so she will not feel lost in communication. We are also committed to building a strong partnership with Anna's family by showing our support. For instance, we plan to have a Portuguese-English bilingual translator/interpreter present when we have the teacher-parent conference with Anna's mom so that we can establish better mutual understanding and communication.

Case Analysis Using the Four Cornerstones of Responsive Practice Framework

Developmentally Responsive Practice

Knowing that Anna needed individualized socioemotional and language support, Ms. Diaz made intentional attempts to do so, such as engaging her in puzzle solving and game playing to help her learn English. All of these activities were appropriate in meeting Anna's learning needs at her developmental level.

Culturally Responsive Practice

Ms. Diaz made a conscious decision to incorporate cultural elements when working with Anna, such as playing Brazilian cultural songs that were familiar to Anna during music time. Songs are an effective mechanism for learning a language and transmitting cultural knowledge such as values and beliefs. Listening to Brazilian cultural songs in the classroom showed respect for Anna's culture, thereby potentially making her feel more comfortable and included. This strategy of care and respect could effectively help cultivate a supportive and trusting relationship between Ms. Diaz and Anna in the classroom and between Ms. Diaz and Anna's family.

Linguistically Responsive Practice

Ms. Diaz made a concerted effort to learn some words in Portuguese to better communicate with Anna and make her and her family feel comfortable and included in a supportive classroom community. Additionally, Ms. Diaz incorporated some children's books written in Portuguese for Anna to read, with English translations for other children to understand. This intentional effort enhanced Anna's learning and her relationship with the other children in the classroom. This approach also showed respect for Anna's native language and support for her native language maintenance. Furthermore, Ms. Diaz also intentionally learned some basic words in Portuguese to communicate with Anna's mom in an effort to establish a strong teacher-family partnership.

Contextually Responsive Practice

Recognizing that children's development occurs in context, Ms. Diaz made a concerted effort to get to know Anna and her family. Some of the contextual knowledge guiding Ms. Diaz's instructional decision included knowing that Anna and her family recently relocated from Brazil, that they only spoke Portuguese fluently, and that her mother used Google Translate to assist with communicating. To establish a partnership with Anna's family, Ms. Diaz recognized that it was important for her not only to help Anna learn English but also to overcome communication barriers with her mom by having a translator/interpreter on hand during their future meetings.

CASE STUDY #3:

Partnering with Parents of a Preschool Child to Help Them Understand the Individualized Education Program (IEP) Process

Samantha Kaufman, Prekindergarten Teacher

Context

I teach in a large diverse urban school district. The sociodemographic information provided by the school district on its website is used here to contextualize the characteristics of the student population. First and foremost, my school district is considered large, with more than 28,000 students, of whom over 3,000 are preschool aged. The school community is made up of a diversity of cultures, backgrounds, languages, and ethnicities: 74 percent of the students are identified as Hispanic, 16 percent as Black, 8 percent as White, and 2 percent as Asian. Forty-six different languages are spoken by the students and their families. Most of the students (80 percent) in the school district are from low-income backgrounds, as indicated by their receiving free or reduced lunches. There are three early childhood centers, twenty-six prekindergarten–eighth grade schools, and eight high schools in this school district.

I have had the pleasure of teaching in one of the ten prekindergarten inclusion classrooms for children with typical educational needs and those with special needs. My classroom consisted of fifteen four- and five-year-olds, two of whom spoke only English, eight spoke Spanish, and five were fluent English-Spanish bilinguals. Of these children, only five of their parents were fluent English-Spanish bilinguals, and ten spoke only Spanish. Two of the children had an IEP for speech. To address the children's bilingual needs, the school district's prekindergarten program was supported by the use of both Spanish and English. For instance, all classroom items and materials were labeled in both languages, books were read in both languages, and at least one of the two teaching staff must speak English and the other Spanish. While teaching a bilingual group of children, I was confronted with some challenges. One of the biggest challenges was explaining to parents why their child would benefit from having an IEP and what an IEP would entail once their child had one.

Case Narrative

Since the start of the school year in September, José, a four-year-old boy, has been exhibiting difficulties in regulating his emotions and behaviors in the classroom. These challenges manifest as impulsivity, defiance, difficulty following instructions, limited language skills to communicate, and instances of physical harm toward himself, his peers, and even me.

Prekindergarten is José's first exposure to a group educational setting. He has two older sisters who attend school in the same district. José lives in a small apartment with his mom, dad, grandma, two older sisters, and a pet dog. His parents and grandma are all bilingual, with Spanish being their first language and English their second. However, they have begun speaking only in English to José at home when they noticed that he wasn't speaking, with the intention of focusing on using the single language, English, that he would need to be successful in school. His grandma shared with me that José's father struggled in school as well. José's mother inquired about the possibility of having José receive special assistance at school, while sharing her concerns with me regarding his speech delay and behavioral challenges. After explaining that students could only receive special services like speech therapy if the district evaluated them as eligible for these services, José's mother wrote a letter to the Division of Special Services requesting José be evaluated.

After months of waiting, evaluating, observing, and working with José on different interventions, in May it was finally time to decide whether José would qualify for special services. Due to the ongoing COVID-19 pandemic, the meeting was held virtually, with only José's father attending in person with the case manager. When the case manager was reading all the reports to José's father, with all the technical language, José's father was a bit confused, had many questions, and was not understanding what was being disclosed to him. He indicated that he would discuss further with José's mother and let the case manager know of their decision on whether they would accept the IEP that the school was proposing for José. I found out the following day that José's parents had denied the IEP for him. Something did not feel right to me, as I knew that José's mother expressed to me all year long that she wanted him to receive help with speech and behavior, so I wondered why they would deny the IEP now. I decided to invite José's mother to talk with me about the meeting and ask any questions that she might have.

When we talked in person, José's mother explained to me that all her husband heard at the meeting was, "Your child will be in special education. He is disabled. He will never be anything in life." I was shocked at how José's father interpreted all the information that was given to him at the meeting. I also felt awful that José's parents only interpreted the negative and not the positive about the IEP for their child. José's mother politely asked me to explain to her what the plan was, and what it would mean for José's future, because in her country, once a child was labeled a "special education" student, there was no turning back, meaning that the child would always be labeled as such and never amount to anything.

I first reassured José's mother that all information related to IEP is strictly confidential and that only his teachers and the professionals involved in delivering the specified services, like the speech therapist, have access to this information, and that others would not know about José's IEP. Additionally, I explained to José's mother what an inclusion classroom would mean for him, in an effort to clarify their original worry that it was the same as a self-contained classroom where he would be placed with only peers with special needs and from whom he could not learn. I also shared with José's mother that our current prekindergarten classroom was an inclusion one, with some students having IEPs. Furthermore, I clarified other terms that the case manager used with José's father at the meeting that the family was unclear about and had concerns with, such as "push-in" and "pull-out."

After meeting for about an hour when I carefully explained to her what the IEP would entail and patiently responded to all her questions and concerns, José's mother expressed appreciation for gaining a better understanding of what an IEP meant and how it could help José if she signed him up for it. She indicated her intention to discuss the matter with José's father and then informed me of their decision. Much to my delight, I received an email from the case manager later that day stating that José's parents had changed their minds and would now like to move forward with the IEP for him.

Case Analysis Using the Four Cornerstones of Responsive Practice Framework

Developmentally Responsive Practice

Ms. Kaufman noticed that José was struggling to exhibit developmentally appropriate behaviors. José's family also noticed similar issues, especially his limited language skills and challenging behaviors at home. Ms. Kaufman offered support to José's parents by suggesting that he undergo evaluation for eligibility to receive special educational services. She also took time to explain to José's mother what it meant for him to receive an IEP. Ms. Kaufman was engaging in developmentally appropriate practices with José by identifying his learning and developmental needs and partnering with his parents to advocate for special educational services for him.

Culturally Responsive Practice

Upon learning about the father's hesitancy to accept an IEP for José as related to a cultural stigma against special education and a concern that the child was being perceived as an incapable human being, Ms. Kaufman made a concerted effort to meet with José's mother to clarify the father's concerns and to better understand their cultural perceptions surrounding the IEP. By explaining the IEP to José's mother and reassuring her of its confidentiality, Ms. Kaufman helped ease her culturally-derived concerns and offered needed support. Learning how cultural differences could hinder effective teacher-family communication, Ms. Kaufman gained a newfound perspective on facilitating open communication as a means to better partner with and support families from other cultural backgrounds.

Linguistically Responsive Practice

Through her conversation with José's mother, Ms. Kaufman learned how language barriers, especially regarding the technical terms used by the case manager, had hampered the father's understanding of the benefits of an IEP for supporting José's language development and behavioral improvement. Ms. Kaufman patiently provided clarifications and addressed José's mother's concerns in a more linguistically friendly manner using language that parents could understand. By engaging in this linguistically responsive practice, Ms. Kaufman started forming a positive partnership with José's family.

Contextually Responsive Practice

By incorporating her knowledge of José's family background and their cultural concerns surrounding the idea of an IEP, Ms. Kaufman began to engage in contextually responsive practice. Specifically, she first sought to understand their specific concerns and then worked to clarify what the case manager was trying to convey to José's father. This contextually responsive approach helped bridge the communication gap between the school and home. It also promoted mutual understanding that helped cultivate a trusting teacher-family partnership dedicated to meeting José's educational needs.

CASE STUDY #4:

It Takes a Village: Scaffolding Two First-Grade DLLs and Partnering with Their Families and Other Educators

Helen Papoutsakis, First-Grade Teacher

Context

I was teaching twenty-three students in my inclusive first-grade class in a middle-income, suburban community. Of the twenty-three students, six were DLLs, five of whom spoke Spanish and one, Arabic. The DLL who spoke Arabic exited the English language learner (ELL) program mid-school year, and my newest Spanish-speaking DLL joined our class toward the end of the school year. Considering that I did not speak the home languages of my DLLs, our communication was challenging as it was restricted to English only.

My five Spanish-speaking DLLs varied in English proficiency level. My newest DLL spoke no English, and two of the other four DLLs were classified as communication impaired in April of their kindergarten school year and were pulled out for literacy and math. The remaining two DLLs (a boy named here as Victor and a girl named here as Marcella) were comfortable speaking English to other students but often struggled with the meaning of words and letter-sound identification, as well as encoding and decoding (writing and reading) consonant-vowel-consonant words. Marcella was repeating first grade due to her below-grade academic performance.

Case Narrative

To scaffold Victor and Marcella in their word comprehension, I applied several strategies, including using visuals (e.g., pictures) to accompany the target words. While the preparation of appropriate visuals was a time-consuming process, I was glad that it helped Victor and Marcella build their vocabulary and comprehension abilities. Additionally, I provided these DLLs with differentiated instruction by regularly pulling them aside for small-group support. During these individualized sessions, we reviewed vocabulary and created vocabulary webs that they could refer to later. To further support Victor and Marcella, I utilized the online platform www.wordwall.net to create interactive games, focusing especially on concept and vocabulary development. Moreover, I engaged them in rhyming games accompanied by visuals to help reinforce their vocabulary building, word meaning, and phonemic awareness. I observed that these various forms of additional support greatly benefited the two DLLs' language learning, as evident in their significant progress in this area.

Partnering with DLLs' Parents

The parents of my DLLs, including Victor and Marcella, had limited English proficiency and spoke exclusively Spanish at home and could not assist their children with homework. Therefore, my DLLs were only exposed to the English language and received educational support in English at school. This issue became evident during an Intervention and referral services meeting when one of the mothers expressed her concern about not being able to read in English to support her child's homework at home. In an effort to communicate with my DLLs' families, I relied on Google Translate to help translate my messages into Spanish. Recognizing that Google Translate might not be accurate, I sought assistance from a Spanish-speaking fellow teacher to proofread the translated messages for accuracy and grammar, thereby ensuring that my Spanish-speaking families would understand these messages well. I noticed that due to language barriers between us, the parents often felt more comfortable reaching out to the ESL teacher who also spoke Spanish and understood their cultural backgrounds. Thus, I shared specific details about particular DLLs with the ESL teacher so that she could relay them to the parents.

Partnering with Other Teachers

Usually our DLLs would need time to learn English and would not be considered for reading intervention immediately. However, because Victor and Marcella were struggling with encoding and decoding, I sought help for them early on by reaching out to the reading interventionist and the ESL teacher at my school and had both students added to their instructional groups. The reading interventionist pulled Victor and Marcella aside into a small group consisting of three to four children for thirty minutes every day. She worked with them on letter sounds and phonemic awareness, as well as encoding and decoding words and sentences. In addition, she reread sentences to help Victor and Marcella build fluency and provided developmentally appropriate books for them to read and decode. The ESL teacher also conducted small-group instruction but had double the number of children than the reading interventionist's group. The ESL teacher focused primarily on building vocabulary and engaging Victor and Marcella in conversation. By the second half of first grade, Victor and Marcella had mastered decoding skills and could read consonant-vowel-consonant words and sentences. However, they continued to struggle with understanding the meaning of words. For example, they could decode the word *mud* but did not know what it meant.

Recognizing the importance of teamwork in the students' education, I maintained collaboration and communication with the ESL teacher and kept her informed about our classroom activities. In turn, she provided additional support to Victor and Marcella by incorporating more vocabulary and visuals into their shared sessions. For instance, when we focused on the topic of nonfiction and animals, she integrated an animal unit into her lessons, ensuring that Victor and Marcella received further exposure to the English language.

It Takes a Village

Through collaborating with other teachers to support the two DLLs, I deepened my appreciation for the power of teamwork. For instance, I collaborated intentionally with the reading interventionist and the ESL teacher (both of whom provided additional instructional support to the DLLs), relied on my fellow teacher for checking my Spanish translations, and partnered with the DLLs' parents. This supportive teamwork enabled me to better serve the needs of my DLL students. However, I found that partnering with the DLLs' families was the most challenging yet rewarding aspect of my role as a teacher. Thus, I am determined to navigate the complexities involved and seek more effective strategies to cultivate stronger connections with my students' families in the future.

Case Analysis Using the Four Cornerstones of Responsive Practice Framework

Developmentally Responsive Practice

Mrs. Papoutsakis demonstrated that she understood her DLLs' actual levels of development, based on which she actively scaffolded their learning to reach their potential levels of development. For instance, recognizing that Victor and Marcella were struggling with encoding and decoding words in English, Mrs. Papoutsakis sought out the reading interventionist to provide extra assistance to these two DLLs. Upon observing Victor's and Marcella's lack of word comprehension, Mrs. Papoutsakis scaffolded their understanding of vocabulary by providing visual accompaniments. Additionally, Mrs. Papoutsakis provided differentiated instruction to Victor and Marcella by creating vocabulary webs and engaging them in interactive learning games.

Culturally Responsive Practice

Capitalizing on her strong understanding of Victor's and Marcella's English language needs, Mrs. Papoutsakis could enhance their learning experiences by incorporating culturally-meaningful activities that would resonate with them. Integrating culturally-relevant learning activities for her DLLs might make them feel more interested and motivated, thereby potentially making the acquisition of complex concepts easier. In the same vein, Mrs. Papoutsakis might also continue collaborating with the ESL teacher to develop culturally-responsive language activities that they both could implement. Furthermore, they could continue exchanging culturally relevant knowledge and strategies to better support the learning and development of the same DLLs they educate.

Linguistically Responsive Practice

Mrs. Papoutsakis collaborated with other teachers (the reading interventionist and the ESL teacher) to provide the responsive support needed to help Victor and Marcella reach grade-level proficiency in English. For instance, the ESL teacher, who was fluent in Spanish, helped Victor and Marcella communicate their understanding. Linguistically responsive practice extends beyond simply offering support in the DLLs' first language to encompass implementing diverse approaches to address their language learning needs. For example, Mrs. Papoutsakis incorporated visual accompaniments to scaffold Victor's and Marcella's understanding of new vocabulary. She also tapped into young children's developmental liking for interactive computer games and rhyming by providing games for the two DLLs to build vocabulary and reinforce language learning. In the future, Mrs. Papoutsakis could also consider encouraging positive transfer of cognitive and language skills from Spanish to English to further facilitate the language learning of DLLs. However, since Mrs. Papoutsakis does not speak Spanish, she may consider relying on the ESL teacher to help implement positive transfer strategies.

Contextually Responsive Practice

The DLLs' developmental levels as well as their linguistic and cultural characteristics are all critical contexts for teachers to consider. In the case of Victor and Marcella, Mrs. Papoutsakis implemented several strategies to support their English language learning, including using visual accompaniments to reinforce understanding of new vocabulary, creating vocabulary webs, and incorporating interactive language learning games both online and offline. Additionally, Mrs. Papoutsakis established effective communication with the families of these children as another essential contextually responsive practice despite finding it challenging due to their language and cultural differences. This phenomenon appears to be a common contextual challenge experienced by many teachers and families who do not share a common language or cultural understanding. Nonetheless, recognizing the importance of strong teacher-family partnerships in children's education, Mrs. Papoutsakis was determined to find ways to better connect with her students' families from different cultural and linguistic backgrounds. One strategy may be to continue collaborating with teachers who speak the home language(s) of the DLLs in her classroom. Furthermore, Mrs. Papoutsakis may also engage in a supportive network with other teachers working with the same DLLs and their families to exchange observations, information, and effective strategies. This collaborative network serves as a valuable place for Mrs. Papoutsakis not only to receive emotional support but also to seize opportunities for professional learning and growth.

Enhancing the Support System to Build Teacher Capacity

Educating young children in general and DLLs in particular is a complex endeavor. Teachers cannot do it alone; they need professional support as much as the DLLs need their instructional support. The following are some ideas for enhancing teachers' support system, which can in turn help build a stronger linguistically and culturally competent teacher workforce to better work with DLLs and their families:

- **Building strong teacher capacity through professional development.** At a time when superdiversity is prominent in early childhood classrooms, teachers must continuously acquire linguistic and cultural competence to enhance their teaching practice. As there is no one dominant non-English language and culture, there may be multiple languages and cultures represented in the classroom. Thus, teachers should engage or continue to engage in ongoing professional development that focuses on building strong or stronger linguistic and cultural competence needed to support the diverse needs of their learners.
- **Assessing DLLs to better understand their learning strengths and needs.** Assessment instruments should consider the diverse learning strengths and needs of DLLs, especially those who speak a low frequency non-English language. For instance, while Spanish has been the dominant minority language assessed in preschool, language proficiency in other languages should also be considered to provide a more comprehensive and responsive education to those DLLs whose home languages are less common, such as Brazilian-style Portuguese in Ms. Diaz's classroom.
- **Implementing policy to build a stronger teacher workforce.** Policy support is needed to provide linguistic and cultural competence training to teachers already in the field. In addition, to build a stronger and more diverse workforce, efforts must be made to identify, recruit, hire, and retain a diverse group of early childhood teachers who understand or have the positive dispositions to learn to deliver developmentally, linguistically, culturally, and contextually responsive educational services to DLLs and their families.
- **Fostering diversity, equity, and inclusion/inclusivity.** Early childhood educators should foster a learning environment and responsive practice that support diversity, equity, and inclusion/inclusivity, thereby empowering DLLs to thrive academically and socially. This approach includes respecting and leveraging the linguistic and cultural backgrounds of DLLs and their families as assets and not liabilities. To begin, teachers should cultivate strong teacher-family partnerships by first establishing positive, respectful, and effective

communication, as demonstrated by Ms. Ahmadein and Ms. Kaufman in their concerted efforts to do so with their DLLs' families.
- **Engaging families to establish strong teacher-family partnerships.** As early childhood educational settings are becoming increasingly superdiverse, school leaders should continuously identify better ways to implement responsive family engagement strategies to bridge the divide between the home and school in the education of DLLs. Considerations include being flexible with the different means of communication as well as translating materials and offering translators/interpreters in outreach efforts to break cultural and linguistic barriers.
- **Creating a culture of teacher-teacher collaboration.** While there may be a main classroom teacher who works directly and mostly with DLLs, some DLLs may also work with other teachers and professionals (e.g., reading interventionist, ESL teacher, special education teacher, speech pathologists, occupational therapists). It is critical that the classroom teacher joins forces with all of these teachers/professionals in collectively supporting the DLLs' learning and developmental needs, as demonstrated by Mrs. Papoutsakis in her collaboration with other educators who were working with the same DLLs.

Chapter Conclusion

This chapter is premised on the idea that child development occurs in context. From the perspective of Bronfenbrenner's (1979) socioecological theory, teachers and parents should work together to establish and maintain strong positive partnerships, especially considering that parents and teachers are two innermost contexts that exert the strongest direct influences on the child's development and learning. It is clear that a critical ingredient of strong teacher-family partnerships is respectful communication. There are various methods of communication through which teachers can effectively engage parents in a collaborative effort to enhance the child's educational journey. First, it is critical that teachers learn about the child's developmental, cultural, linguistic, and contextual backgrounds. This information can, in turn, help them better respond to the child's developmental and learning needs, as demonstrated by the case studies featured in this chapter. When teachers, other educators, and parents work together, the child's education will likely benefit.

7 | Building Strong Teacher-Family and Teacher-Teacher Partnerships

Reflection Questions

- How have you established or how might you establish positive teacher-family partnerships?

- What challenges and/or opportunities have you encountered or might you envision encountering in establishing teacher-family partnerships?

CHAPTER 8

Supporting Learners with Special Needs

You are a very special person. There is only one like you in the whole world. There's never been anyone exactly like you before, and there will never be again.

—Fred Rogers, host, creator, and writer of the children's television series *Mister Rogers' Neighborhood*

Fred Rogers's quote reminds us to treat children as "very special" people with unique strengths, characteristics, and needs. Furthermore, just like the developmentally appropriate practice framework that NAEYC (2020) advocated, children share both commonalities and individualities. Developmentally, some children are advanced and talented in certain areas, some are average, and others experience various challenges that require the support of special educational services in addressing their specific learning and/or developmental needs.

Just like the general population, the DLL population also contains some who are diagnosed with neurodevelopmental disorders (e.g., attention deficit hyperactivity disorder, autism, obsessive-compulsive disorder) and disabilities (e.g., speech or language impairment). Thus, teachers need to be equipped with the appropriate knowledge, skills, and dispositions to serve DLLs' special developmental and learning needs, while recognizing and incorporating their bilingual and bicultural characteristics in the process.

Special Education and Related Services

In their *Report on the Condition of Education 2023*, Véronique Irwin and colleagues (2023) noted the following:

- The number of students ages three to twenty-one who received special education and related services under the Individuals with Disabilities Education Act (IDEA) increased significantly from 6.4 million in the 2010–11 school year to 7.3 million in the 2021–22 school year.
- These students encompassed various disability[1] categories, with the largest percentages falling into specific learning disabilities (that is, lacking ability areas such as speaking, writing, and doing mathematical calculations) (32 percent); speech or language impairment (19 percent); other health impairment (15 percent); and autism (12 percent).
- Among the proportions of students served under IDEA relative to the total public school enrollment in pre-K–12, the highest percentages were observed among American Indian/Alaska Native students (19 percent) and Black students (17 percent), with the lowest percentages among Pacific Islander students (11 percent) and Asian students (8 percent).

While these data provide valuable insights into the overall student population, they are not separated by age group, thereby providing no clear understanding concerning the early childhood population.

In its analysis based on the data from the 2018–19 school year, the Office of Special Education Programs (OSEP 2020) reported some salient findings regarding children ages three to five who were receiving special education and related services under IDEA in the United States and outlying areas:

- Of children in this age group, 6.75 percent were served under IDEA.
- A majority of those receiving special services under IDEA were boys, accounting for 69.47 percent.
- The largest proportion of children in this group receiving special services was identified as White (50.61 percent), followed by Hispanic/Latino (26.53 percent) and Black or African American (12.86 percent). The smallest percentage belonged to two or more races (4.46 percent), Asian (4.08 percent), and American Indian or Alaska Native (1.17 percent).

---

1. While the federal IDEA has been using the term *disabilities*, it is important to recognize that it tends to carry negative connotations. Thus, educators need to be sensitive to these negative connotations and show respect to individuals with disabilities. Instead of using the term *individuals with disabilities*, the term *individuals with exceptionalities* has been used by some to highlight differences and strengths rather than purely disabilities. A respectful approach is to ask the person with disability or disabilities directly what language term they would prefer you to use in describing them.

- A significant proportion of this child population (45.5 percent) received most of their special services under IDEA within their regular early childhood programs, followed by 24.6 percent in some alternative locations; 21.7 percent in separate special education classes, schools, or residential facilities; 6.3 percent in service provider locations or some other settings; and the lowest percentage (1.9 percent) in the home.
- In the 2018–19 school year, 8.43 percent of all children ages three to five or preschool years with disabilities served under IDEA were identified as English language learners (ELLs). This particular finding underscores the intersectionality of language needs and special education or related services for young children who are diagnosed with disabilities during these preschool years and are likely to benefit from early intervention. Additionally, some young children have not yet been diagnosed. In the 2018–19 school year, there was also a significantly large percentage (45.5 percent) of the child population (ages three to five) receiving most of their special services under IDEA within their regular, inclusive early childhood programs. Thus, many of these classrooms are not only superdiverse *across* but also *within* the various DLL groups experiencing common or different disabilities.

A student diagnosed with a disability or disabilities may receive special education and special services through an individualized education program/plan (IEP) that is proposed by their Child Study Team, comprising a multidisciplinary group of professionals who must receive consent from the child's parents. The IEP involves "a written statement for each child with a disability that is developed, reviewed, and revised in a meeting" that includes a plan for addressing and meeting the special needs of the child to achieve annual goals as delineated (IDEA 2017, n.p.). Other students may be eligible to receive a 504 plan, which requires educational institutions "to provide to students with disabilities appropriate educational services designed to meet the individual needs of such students to the same extent as the needs of students without disabilities are met. . . . [consisting] of education in regular classrooms, education in regular classes with supplementary services, and/or special education and related services" (US Department of Education, accessed 2024, n.p.). While there is federal guidance regarding procedures and provision of special educational services through an IEP or a 504 plan, there are also state-specific stipulations and process mechanisms.

The seemingly ever-growing DLL population brings valuable linguistic and cultural strengths to the classroom. Yet it also poses tremendous challenges for teachers, especially in tackling the diverse learning and developmental needs of those DLLs who require early intervention and other special educational services. What follows are four case studies that demonstrate possibilities for supporting DLLs with special needs. They are analyzed using the Four Cornerstones of Responsive Practice Framework.

CASE STUDY #1:

What It Means to Teach Preschool Children with Special Needs
Tiffany Enciso-Williams, Former Preschool Special Education Teacher

Context
I hold a teaching certification in early childhood special education, and for the last couple of years, I was working as a preschool special education teacher in a school district in a middle-class neighborhood. I taught in a classroom of about ten children ages three to four who were identified as having delays in multiple developmental areas and needing extra support. We had about eight preschool classes at our school, and because I was one of the two teachers at the school who spoke Spanish, my class often had a higher number of children who were bilingual, specifically English and Spanish. Growing up in a bilingual household myself, I have always appreciated the importance of staying connected to one's culture and family through language and of preserving one's culture and language by passing them down.

Case Narrative
The biggest hurdle I faced while working with DLLs at this particular school was feeling like I did not have the resources to fully support their learning and development. Because I was able to speak Spanish, I felt satisfied that I could help many exclusively Spanish-speaking families navigate the paperwork and the world of special education, but in the classroom, I always felt like more could be done. One situation that I remember involved a student who spoke both English and Spanish. She was attending our program to support her speech delay, and when she spoke, it was often difficult to decipher whether she was saying something in English or in Spanish, or what exactly she was trying to tell us. I remember one time, this

student was playing in the toy kitchen area and naming pretend foods as she played, saying *"huevo"* while playing with an egg. The classroom aide at the time then held the pretend egg up and started repeating "egg" multiple times, wanting her to repeat the word in English. I walked over and validated that the student was in fact saying *egg*, but in Spanish. This, of course, is just one example and not indicative of every interaction. But during my time teaching at this school, I did feel like there was a lack of training on the benefits of bilingualism and how to best support the DLLs' learning needs in the classroom.

As another of my students with a mild speech delay transitioned from my class to a bilingual kindergarten class, a staff member commented, "Now he is going to be even more confused." A lack of information and appreciation of bilingualism, and maybe even a lack of diversity of languages spoken by the staff at the school site, could all be contributing factors. I have always encouraged families to continue speaking to their children in their home language. School should be a place of celebration, not assimilation. Yet, especially when speech delays are present, parents can be scared of "confusing" the child or may want the child to "catch up" in English before they learn another language. I always wondered why the topic of bilingualism was not a bigger point of discussion among the speech pathologists at my school site as they sought to support families to enhance their child's language and speech. By sharing proper information, these families may have felt better supported.

Case Analysis Using the Four Cornerstones of Responsive Practice Framework

Developmentally Responsive Practice

Ms. Enciso-Williams's reflection on her work with DLLs with special needs serves as an important reminder of some critical issues that the early childhood education field should consider addressing. These issues include teachers' attitudes toward, knowledge about, and support for the bilingual development of DLLs, especially those with special needs. While it is already challenging for DLLs to navigate learning a new language and culture, it is even more challenging for DLLs with special needs to navigate the additional hurdles that come with their special conditions. Teachers should receive adequate professional development in recognizing the challenges facing DLLs with special needs to better support their bilingual development as well as their individual learning and developmental needs.

Culturally Responsive Practice

Ms. Enciso-Williams's reflection on her school site where bilingualism was seemingly not promoted suggests that there is a critical need for teachers to engage in professional development to learn to better support the language learning and developmental needs of DLLs in the classroom. When they lack cultural knowledge concerning their DLLs, educators are less able to engage in culturally responsive practice. Thus, it is important that educators are willing to learn about their DLLs' cultural backgrounds. They can then incorporate the knowledge gained to orchestrate culturally responsive learning experiences for these DLLs.

Linguistically Responsive Practice

Ms. Enciso-Williams reflected on the usefulness of leveraging her Spanish-English bilingual abilities to help Spanish-speaking families understand the information conveyed to them, including details about special education. Furthermore, her observation of the classroom aide not understanding a child's non-English language to provide appropriate linguistic and cognitive validation demonstrates a critical need in the field. That is, in classrooms where there are DLLs, it is particularly beneficial to have a bilingual teacher or assistant teacher who can speak the home language of these DLLs to establish better understanding and validation of as well as support for their cultural and linguistic strengths. Furthermore, they can also leverage the common underlying proficiency principle (as discussed in chapter 4) to facilitate positive transfer of knowledge and skills between the home language and English if possible. In classrooms where the teacher and assistant teacher do not speak the home language of the DLLs, they might make a concerted effort to familiarize themselves with aspects of these learners' language and culture. Incorporating this knowledge into their work with DLLs is critical to supporting DLLs' learning and development. Some teachers may even take the initiative to research or learn some commonly used words in the DLLs' home language to incorporate into their communication with the DLLs.

Contextually Responsive Practice

Ms. Enciso-Williams's reflection on the issues related to the teachers' lack of knowledge of and appreciation for the values of bilingualism underscores yet another critical need for educators to understand and view bilingual abilities as assets and not liabilities. For example, the lack of understanding might lead educators to scale back on promoting bilingual development in DLLs with speech delays to avoid language confusion. While speech delays are a cause for concern, educators and speech pathologists alike should evaluate whether such an issue occurs in DLLs' L1, L2, or both. Such contextual information will enable professionals to provide better targeted support accordingly.

CASE STUDY #2:

Supporting a DLL's Acquisition of Language Skills in a Self-Contained Classroom

Erin Vaccaro, Preschool-Kindergarten Special Education Teacher

Context

I teach children from preschool through kindergarten in a multiage, self-contained special education classroom in a public school. In my classroom, four children with IEPs are taught by a teaching team consisting of myself as the lead teacher and three paraprofessionals. Although the school is located in a small, affluent suburban community comprising mostly upper-middle-class families, three of the four children in my class qualify for the free and reduced lunch program. All four children have immigrant parents, originating in the following countries: Georgia, Costa Rica, Mexico, China, and Iran. Accordingly, English, Farsi, Spanish, or Georgian is spoken by each of these families at home.

To be eligible for placement in the self-contained class, the children must demonstrate both cognitive and significant language impairments. To communicate, two of the children use single words, while the other two are nonverbal and rely on augmentative or alternative communication. The initial eligibility testing for all four children was conducted exclusively in English per their parents' request. Since testing was solely conducted in English, the assessment of receptive language skills in the child's non-English home language is left to the discretion of the teacher and speech therapist.

Case Narrative

Daniel, a three-year-old boy, is one of the two nonverbal children in my class. He is currently classified as "a preschool child with a disability." This is Daniel's first experience in a school setting. Prior, he received only limited in-home early intervention services with a speech and language pathologist. He lives with his mother and his eight-year-old sister. Although Daniel's mother speaks Mandarin Chinese as her first language, she predominantly speaks Spanish in the home. Daniel's father currently lives in Mexico, where his parents originally met. Daniel's older sister is fluent in Spanish and English, while his mother does not consider herself fluent in English. All written communication sent home is translated into Spanish by a translator. Daniel's mother has expressed that although she prefers correspondence in Spanish, she is open to communication in English.

The meetings between the school's Child Study Team and Daniel's mother to review his IEP progress were conducted in English. Even though a translator was offered for all the meetings, Daniel's mother declined the offer. When Daniel started school in my classroom, his language skills were assessed as being significantly delayed for his age. Since Daniel could not produce any words or word approximations, his academic as well as language and social skills were all assessed receptively (based on what he could understand from what was communicated to him verbally).

During the first week of school, Daniel demonstrated his ability to recognize all uppercase and lowercase letters, numbers 1–30, ten colors, and eight basic two-dimensional shapes. Daniel was also assessed for his ability to imitate simple gross-motor actions, including clapping hands, touching his nose, and stomping his feet. While he successfully imitated all gross-motor movements when provided with visual prompts, he was unable to execute the same actions solely based on verbal cues. To determine whether this problem was a skill issue or a result of a language barrier, my Spanish-speaking paraprofessional repeated the targeted list of skills in Spanish. The assessment revealed that most of the missing skills could be attributed to Daniel's unfamiliarity with the English terminology, as he was able to understand the terms when said in Spanish.

The assessment of Daniel's language skills prompted us to initiate the applied behavior analysis (ABA) program for him. When facilitating language development, ABA practitioners in my program employ B. F. Skinner's verbal operants and streamline instructions when a learner encounters difficulty. For example, if a child is struggling with the verbal instruction "Go to your cubby and bring back your lunch box," an ABA practitioner can then simplify the instruction to "Go get lunch box," accompanied by a gesture prompt directed toward the cubby. Because we are trained to simplify language, many teachers do not typically consider incorporating or modifying a directive in a different language.

To address Daniel's learning needs, I encourage my Spanish-speaking paraprofessional to repeat the instruction in Spanish, a language that Daniel mainly understands. For instance, one time we engaged Daniel in an activity involving learning the body parts through using gross-motor skills in action. When the paraprofessional said, "Touch your nose" and Daniel incorrectly touched his ears, she would then prompt him with *"Touch nariz."* This kind of bilingual instruction is not generally emphasized as a method in the ABA literature, but it has been proven effective for enhancing Daniel's understanding.

Furthermore, given that Daniel is able to understand mainly Spanish at this point, I encourage my paraprofessionals to play or model language in both Spanish and English for Daniel during other learning activities, such as facilitated play. For instance, a paraprofessional enjoys playing in the toy kitchen/restaurant area with Daniel, including pretending to order cupcakes. Since the toy cupcakes come in different colors, the paraprofessional orders the different-colored cupcakes using the Spanish words for each color.

To promote cultural understanding, we incorporate lessons on holidays during our large-group time. For instance, during National Hispanic Heritage Month, we read several books including *Round Is a Tortilla*, *¡Me gusta cómo soy! (I Like Myself)*, *Pepe and the Parade*, and *Día de los Muertos*. Reading these cultural books seemed to have promoted Daniel's learning engagement because they were relatable to his Hispanic culture and the Spanish language.

Case Analysis Using the Four Cornerstones of Responsive Practice Framework

Developmentally Responsive Practice

Ms. Vaccaro engaged Daniel in various learning activities that were developmentally appropriate for children his age. In addition, recognizing that Daniel was a nonverbal child, Ms. Vaccaro employed action-based activities to enable him to physically demonstrate his understanding of directions, concepts, and actions, such as touching his nose. In Daniel's unique situation, this nonverbal communication approach was developmentally appropriate. Furthermore, instead of simplifying language as part of what traditional ABA programs would do, Ms. Vaccaro encouraged her Spanish-speaking paraprofessional to use Spanish to communicate with and teach Daniel, who understood mainly Spanish. This method was found helpful to Daniel's learning and understanding of instructions.

Culturally Responsive Practice

To promote cultural understanding, one of Ms. Vaccaro's major strategies was reading books. She identified books related to Hispanic culture or involving the Spanish language that Daniel was likely to resonate with. In doing so, Daniel seemed to have become more engaged and motivated in learning.

Linguistically Responsive Practice

As a monolingual English speaker, Ms. Vaccaro realized that she couldn't effectively communicate with Daniel, who understood primarily Spanish. However, she encouraged her Spanish-speaking paraprofessional to reiterate instructions, concepts, and actions in Spanish. In turn, this effort led to Daniel's understanding of certain instructions, as demonstrated by his relevant actions in response.

Contextually Responsive Practice

Ms. Vaccaro capitalized on her contextual knowledge of Daniel's situation to provide individualized support. For example, recognizing that Daniel was nonverbal and that he understood mainly Spanish, Ms. Vaccaro encouraged her paraprofessional to restate instructions and words in Spanish to promote Daniel's learning and understanding. She continued to encourage her paraprofessional to engage Daniel in Spanish in other learning areas, such as facilitated play. These efforts demonstrate that Ms. Vaccaro sought to understand the contextual factors (such as linguistic and cultural) that shaped Daniel's learning strengths and special needs. Guided by the insights gained, Ms. Vaccaro learned to serve Daniel's special needs in a contextually responsive manner.

CASE STUDY #3:

Supporting the Communication Needs of Three DLLs in a Prekindergarten Self-Contained Classroom

Lissette Y. Ruiz, Prekindergarten Teacher

Context

I am an English-Spanish bilingual, teaching in a prekindergarten self-contained classroom [with only children diagnosed with special needs] in a large urban school district. This school district is considered a primarily low-income community with a high density of residents from various South American and Caribbean countries. At the preschool level, we use the Tools of the Mind curriculum. However, there is no actual curriculum that specifically caters to DLLs' language needs. Teachers have to inquire with families via a home language survey. This survey consists of questions such as "What language is spoken to the child at home?" and "What language does the student speak at home?" Once the child is determined as being qualified for language monitoring and assessment, it becomes the teacher's responsibility not only to monitor and assess the child's English language abilities but also to incorporate various activities and methods to support the child's acquisition of the English language. In my classroom, I teach twelve children (ages three to four), all of whom have an IEP. In addition to my teaching, the children are supported by two paraprofessionals. Here I present three case students who are DLLs to illustrate the similar or different strategies that I use to work with them to address their specific learning and developmental needs.

Case Child #1: Jules

Jules is three years and two months old. He has been diagnosed with autism spectrum disorder and is nonverbal. He is in my middle cognitive functioning group. Per the home language survey by his parents, Jules understands Spanish and is spoken to primarily in this language at home. His family comes from the Dominican Republic. Jules is new to the preschool setting and has only been learning English in school for two months. To support Jules's learning and development, we (the two paraprofessionals and I) communicate with him using American Sign Language (ASL) and a visual board with various basic forms of expression, ranging from "yes/no" to "How are you feeling?" When answering a question or needing assistance, Jules is encouraged to point to the preferred visual to communicate with us. Given that Jules comes from a Spanish-speaking background, we make sure to say the words that he is trying to communicate in both English and Spanish. This approach allows Jules to learn to internalize the words and express himself using these words. During the parent-teacher conference, I informed Jules's parents of the visual supports that are being utilized in the classroom for him, and they were eager to create their own visual boards to reinforce this developmentally appropriate method of communicating his wants and needs.

Case Child #2: Yaz

Yaz is three years and ten months old. She has delays in speech and cognitive processing and is primarily nonverbal. She is in my middle cognitive functioning group. As per the home language survey completed by her parents, Yaz understands and is spoken to in Spanish by her parents but is spoken to in both English and Spanish by her older brother. Yaz's family comes from the Dominican Republic. To support Yaz's learning and development in communicating her wants and needs, we (the two paraprofessionals and I) model the use of ASL and provide a basic visual communication board. Additionally, we encourage gestures as the last resort for Yaz to communicate her wants and needs. Given that Yaz comes from a Spanish-speaking background, we make sure to first say the words that she is trying to communicate in both English and Spanish, and then ask her to try and repeat the word or expression as best as she can. After a few one-on-one sessions with the speech therapist and our consistent reinforcements of using language to communicate, Yaz is now utilizing ASL only as a secondary method of communication with us. When she uses ASL to communicate with us, we are diligent in providing the vocabulary in both English and Spanish to accompany what she is trying to express. At times, Yaz does try to repeat our words in both English and Spanish. The incorporation of ASL into Yaz's means of communication has proven so effective that she has adopted it for use at home as well. During the parent-teacher conference, Yaz's parents inquired about the gestures that Yaz was using with them at home. I explained and demonstrated how we used ASL with Yaz in the classroom. Additionally, I provided them with resources teaching the basic signs that they could practice using with Yaz at home. Yaz's parents were excited to try a new way to support Yaz's communication attempts at home.

Case Child #3: Luke

Luke is five years and five months old. His family comes from Mexico. Luke has speech and language impairment along with challenging behaviors. While he is verbal, Luke's speech is difficult to understand. Luke is in my cognitively high-functioning group and tends to understand and speak using English more than his fellow DLL peers. When working with Luke, I use the Tools of the Mind curriculum to promote language and literacy development. This curriculum was provided by the school district with flexibility for teachers to modify as needed, especially when working with children with special needs. My challenge in working with Luke is that when he is excited, he speaks rapidly, making it very difficult for me to understand what he is trying to communicate. Furthermore, I also notice that Luke mumbles his words, making it even more difficult for me to understand his speech. When I do understand some of his speech, I notice that he communicates using both English and Spanish words in one sentence. To support Luke's efforts to communicate and provide opportunities for him to practice communicating more effectively by slowing down his speech, I remind him to first take three deep breaths, think about what he wants to say before saying it, and then think about which language he would like to use. After Luke has followed these three steps in expressing his needs or wants in his preferred language, I then confirm with him what he has said in that particular language and provide its translation in the other language to support his bilingual development. Most of the time, Luke is successful in using these methods to learn to speak more clearly and slowly. However, due to his challenging behaviors, Luke often needs prompting or redirection. Nonetheless, since the beginning of the school year, he has slowly but surely made noticeable progress in listening, understanding, and speaking using English.

Case Analysis Using the Four Cornerstones of Responsive Practice Framework

Developmentally Responsive Practice

It was evident that Mrs. Ruiz understood the three case DLLs' learning and developmental needs and followed their IEPs as she applied responsive strategies accordingly. For instance, Mrs. Ruiz leveraged ASL and used a visual board as developmentally responsive strategies to support Jules and Yaz in learning to communicate.

Culturally Responsive Practice

Although Mrs. Ruiz did not mention any culturally specific strategies that she used to address the three DLLs' language and speech needs, she was aware of these children's cultural backgrounds. After presenting her three case studies and upon reflecting on her teaching strategies, Mrs. Ruiz shared with me that she was now considering incorporating culturally relevant songs and rhymes in working with these DLLs with special needs.

Linguistically Responsive Practice

Mrs. Ruiz understood the three case DLLs came from Spanish-English bilingual backgrounds. However, given that Jules and Yaz (who were nonverbal) lacked expressive language abilities, they were not able to use the two languages themselves to communicate. Nonetheless, Mrs. Ruiz tried to facilitate their language understanding in both English and Spanish by using these two languages with them in addition to ASL. This strategy could help the two children build receptive language abilities. Furthermore, Mrs. Ruiz made a concerted effort to speak with Luke (who was verbal) in both Spanish and English, as he was more able to understand and communicate using language.

Contextually Responsive Practice

By understanding the contextual needs of the three case DLLs through their IEPs and the neurodevelopmental challenges facing them, Mrs. Ruiz engaged in contextually responsive practice according to their specific needs. For instance, when she was working with Luke, who tended to speak fast when excited, Mrs. Ruiz taught him to follow a three-step process: taking deep breaths, thinking before speaking, and planning which language to use instead of mumbling and intermixing both languages.

CASE STUDY #4:

Supporting the Learning of DLLs with Special Needs
Vanessa Casella, Former Third-Grade Teacher

Context

I previously taught a third-grade class in an urban school community serving children from low-income backgrounds, as indicated by the majority (79 percent) of the student population being eligible for free/reduced lunches. The class consisted of twenty-two children, with eighteen of them progressing academically at grade level and four who were DLLs enrolled in the English Language Learners program where they received separate English instruction from another teacher. Five children in the class had either an IEP or a 504 plan tailored to their specific disabilities and needs. The children's diagnosed disabilities include attention deficit hyperactivity disorder (ADHD) and speech delays. Furthermore, language-wise, the majority of the children (twenty out of twenty-two) were bilingual in Spanish and English. As a Spanish-English bilingual myself, I was able to communicate effectively with these children and their families in Spanish.

Case Narrative

When planning and delivering a lesson, I had to make sure that all the children were grasping it at their own pace and in culturally and linguistically appropriate ways. For example, one of my favorite lessons that I taught in the beginning of the school year was the reading of a storybook called *Gary the Dreamer*, of which all children received a hard copy. The children could also listen to a digital read-aloud online. I chose this story particularly because it resonated with all the children, especially the DLLs. This story, narrated by Gary, was about why he decided to become a writer. The setting of this story also reflected the neighborhood in which the children lived, which was near a city. The children enjoyed the story because they shared common ground with Gary. For example, in the town where my school was located, some people had small houses and some lived in apartment buildings, but they could simply walk a block and get to experience all kinds of cultures when entering the local street markets. My DLLs seemed to like the story a lot because they too understood what it was like to live in a suburb and be so close to an urban area. They also resonated with Gary, who experienced difficulties with learning new things such as a new language. Some of these DLLs understood the feelings Gary had when learning a new language, finding new friends, and understanding a new culture.

This story also discussed different cultures, which reminded the children that even though we might all speak or learn to speak the same language of English, our heritage cultures could all be different. Furthermore, the DLLs working on a lesson together could translate Spanish words for one another. For instance, I would partner children, making sure that there was a child who could speak both Spanish and English. When a DLL did not understand a word or phrase, if I was not available to answer the question(s) right away, a linguistically more advanced DLL peer from the group would help the DLL out. This process made all the children feel confident and motivated in learning.

To support children with learning disabilities, I made sure to adopt appropriate accommodations according not only to their IEPs but also to how they would learn. If I saw that a DLL was not understanding a word or a phrase in the story even if it was translated and explained, I would stop and think of another way to help this child understand the material. In one case, I had one child who would constantly repeat what the other children were saying. At first, I thought this child was doing that to get attention, but then I later learned from talking with him that repetitive speech was the only way he could practice the acquired knowledge and skills. With this new information, I intentionally developed a new lesson to help not only this child but also other DLLs memorize material such as new vocabulary words. For instance, we would sing the word, read it, and even act it out. These learning activities promoted high levels of active participation from all children, especially those with ADHD, who were now able to focus more.

When I was working with my Spanish-English DLLs who had special needs, I recognized the significance of closely observing their unique learning styles and adapting my lessons accordingly to cater to their individual needs. Throughout the academic year when I taught this third-grade class, I was delighted to witness the learning progress that each child made as a result of the individualized instruction and support I provided.

Case Analysis Using the Four Cornerstones of Responsive Practice Framework

Developmentally Responsive Practice

Mrs. Casella made intentional efforts to observe and understand the special needs of her DLLs and adapt her teaching strategies accordingly to meet their individual developmental and learning needs. She provided an example of creating a new developmentally appropriate lesson after learning that one DLL was using repetitive speech as a way to practice what he was learning. Furthermore, Mrs. Casella implemented other strategies, including singing the word, reading it, and acting it out to help DLLs, especially those with ADHD, remember this newly learned vocabulary word.

Culturally Responsive Practice

Gary the Dreamer was a culturally responsive children's book for the DLLs because the story showed respect for different cultures. This content could potentially empower the DLLs to develop cultural awareness, empathy, and understanding, knowing that even though they were all learning English, many came from different cultural backgrounds and all possessed unique cultural characteristics.

Linguistically Responsive Practice

By using the book *Gary the Dreamer*, Mrs. Casella helped her DLLs make connections between Gary's (the main character in the book) difficulty in learning something new and their own efforts in learning a new language and culture as well as making new friends. Accordingly, the challenges experienced by Gary resonated with Mrs. Casella's DLLs. Mrs. Casella also applied the strategy of having her Spanish-English DLLs work together and translate words for one another to help them feel confident and motivated in learning both Spanish and English.

Contextually Responsive Practice

Gary the Dreamer was a contextually responsive book that Mrs. Casella chose for her DLLs because it resonated with them as they made connections between the story and their own backgrounds. For instance, Gary's neighborhood was similar to that of these DLLs, located in a suburb but very close to an urban area. Thus, the story was contextually relatable to the DLLs, helping to empower and motivate them to learn English and acquire language skills. Furthermore, Mrs. Casella adapted her lessons according to the DLLs' special needs, such as those related to ADHD.

Strategies to Support DLLs with Special Needs

The cases narrated by the four early childhood teachers (Ms. Enciso-Williams, Ms. Vaccaro, Mrs. Ruiz, and Mrs. Casella) in this chapter highlight both the challenges and opportunities for supporting the learning and development of DLLs with special needs. They described the developmentally, culturally, linguistically, and contextually responsive strategies they implemented to provide the needed support. In my article with Suzanne Shire, "Strategic Teaching: Fostering Communication Skills in Diverse Young Learners" in *Young Children*, we delineated other responsive strategies to support children with special needs (Chen and Shire 2011, 25):

- Ask a child who has strong academic, linguistic, and/or social competence to assist or be a model. For example, as children sort items by shape, Jacob says to Julie, "Let's find triangles first. They have three sides." He gathers triangles, and Julie follows his lead, noting the attributes of triangles.
- Build on children's strengths and interests when they are acquiring new skills and knowledge. For example, Donald enjoys physical activity and tends to avoid activities related to math concepts. Invite Donald to toss a stack of beanbags into a container, then ask him whether there are more beanbags in the container or outside of it. Help him count the two sets to confirm his answer. Encourage him to continue playing the game and comparing the results.
- Share observations and exchange strategies with other teachers and the support team. For example, schedule frequent meetings with team members to discuss and assess how the strategies work for Ben's learning and to identify other appropriate strategies to support his progress.
- Foster an environment and culture that respects and supports differences in learners. For example, start the year by asking children what their favorite color, activity, or book is and why, and then discuss with the children the similarities and differences in their choices. Read aloud a book, for example *Cleversticks* or *Crow Boy*, about children with different strengths and abilities. After reading, discuss with the children what it is like to be or feel different and how and why they should respect differences in people. Ask them to think of examples from their own experience.

Chapter Conclusion

The statistics suggest there are many students (ages three to twenty-one) in the US education system diagnosed with various types of disabilities (Irwin et al. 2023). Most noticeably, there is a significant percentage of children in the preschool population (ages three to five) requiring special educational services, and among these children, a large proportion of them are English language learners (OSEP 2020). The IEP is a well recognized mechanism for providing special education and services to students with disabilities. While some DLLs have diagnosed disabilities and are receiving special educational services through their IEPs, other DLLs exhibit challenging behaviors that may or may not be related to language issues. Furthermore, while children with special needs may present challenges for teachers, this special population also presents opportunities for teachers to be creative and adaptive, putting their knowledge, skills, and dispositions to the test. Thus, there is a great need for educators to provide targeted guidance and appropriate interventions as necessary to address the special needs of all children, especially DLLs. To better prepare educators for this vital task of supporting DLLs with special needs, theoretical insights and practical resources will continue to be needed for guiding teachers as they seek to better understand and address the diverse learning and developmental needs of this special population.

Reflection Questions

- How have you addressed or how might you address the special needs of DLLs?
- What have been or might be the challenges and opportunities for you in working with DLLs with special needs?

CHAPTER 9

Conclusion: Heart Work and Hard Work

Who dares to teach must never cease to learn.
—John Cotton Dana, library and museum director

As I reflect on my work as a teacher educator and professor of early childhood education who has helped prepare hundreds of pre-service and in-service early childhood teachers in New Jersey for nearly two decades, John Dana's simple yet profound message resonates powerfully with me. In particular, the interplay between teaching and learning continues to fuel my professional growth and purpose to inspire aspiring educators. It also affirms my resolve to remain a lifelong learner, deeply engaged in the discovery of new knowledge to integrate in my own teaching—where learning is at the heart of it all. By sharing my ideas accumulated and brewed over the years through not only my own teaching journey but also my own research on teaching and student learning, as well as infusing some early childhood teachers' authentic voices, I hope this book offers both inspiration and aspiration for all prospective and practicing teachers. The very reason you are reading this book may be because you also desire to keep on learning and to refine the craft of your own teaching.

The Four Cornerstones of Responsive Practice as both a theoretical and practical framework (as described in detail in chapter 5) is made concrete through the reflective case narratives by the teachers in chapters 6–8. The case studies are meant to be descriptive in nature, depicting critical yet likely common challenges and opportunities facing early childhood educators in their teaching practices with culturally and linguistically diverse learners, reflecting the increasing superdiversity in the US student population (as discussed in chapter 3). These practices include responsive strategies the teachers have implemented in three key areas: teacher scaffolding (chapter 6); partnering with children, their families, and other educators (chapter 7); and supporting DLLs with special needs (chapter 8). The situations and strategies discussed may resonate with you and other educators. Specifically, by studying and analyzing the cases through my Four Cornerstones of Responsive Practice framework, educators may find them more easily relatable and see responsive practice in action more concretely, such as in the context of teachers scaffolding DLLs in acquiring receptive and expressive language skills interwoven with BICS and CALP (as discussed in chapter 4).

The Four Cornerstones framework suggests that by investing time and thought in understanding DLLs and their families, teachers can create effective pedagogical strategies that are developmentally, culturally, linguistically, and contextually responsive to their needs. Furthermore, it is perhaps not difficult to see that when teachers care about their students and their learning, these students will likely feel emotionally connected. For instance, when teachers make the curricular content, lessons, and learning activities meaningful to their DLLs' life experiences, these students will likely feel connected to learning and become more motivated and engaged in the learning process.

By analyzing the case narratives through the lens of the Four Cornerstones of Responsive Practice framework, the key idea of connection emerges: teacher-student connections and teacher-family connections. Connecting with others is fundamental to human existence. It is evident that the early childhood teachers whose voices are heard in part 2 of this book have made concerted efforts to build connections with the DLLs and their families from a place of positivity that respects their cultural and linguistic backgrounds as strengths. These positive connections, in turn, have helped unlock the DLLs' learning motivation and engagement and build positive teacher-family partnerships. Furthermore, the circumstances under which the teachers established these professional connections reflect their intentional application of the four elements of responsive practice as described. In essence, they also highlight the teachers' continual professional learning and development through their dedication to reflecting on and improving their practices with culturally and linguistically diverse learners. However, just as DLLs require teacher support, teachers also need support from their school administrators and leaders, including professional development opportunities and trainings that equip them with effective strategies to serve the diverse cultural and linguistic needs of the DLLs as well as those with special needs by incorporating knowledge of their developmental characteristics and contextual circumstances.

While the case narratives in this book are not meant to cover an exhaustive range of topics, they focus on some critical issues and ideas most germane to teaching DLLs. Thus, they may be used by early childhood educators as a *backboard* that supports developmentally, culturally, linguistically, and contextually responsive practice. They may also be used as a *springboard* into self-reflection and self-study by early childhood educators, such as prompting them to critically scrutinize and question the theory governing their own teaching practice as discussed in chapter 2.

As you may agree, teaching is no easy feat. It is a complex process that involves numerous factors, such as knowledge of the subject matter, lesson planning, pedagogical strategies, classroom management, and student assessments. In addition, early childhood teachers working with DLLs and their families must consider other factors affecting the children's educational experiences, such as their cultural and linguistic backgrounds. Thus, there is no single litmus test to account for all the complexities and nuances of teaching effectiveness as a whole. Instead, teaching effectiveness requires a continuous process of reflection to better and more flexibly support the vast facets of children's learning and development. Not surprisingly, my research (Chen 2022) has demonstrated that reflection is necessary for teachers to develop adaptive expertise and pedagogical adaptability (as discussed in chapter 2).

I now conclude this book with some encouraging words, to show my appreciation for the unwavering dedication of many educators (as those whose voices are amplified in this book) vested in the learning and success of all children, especially DLLs. I firmly believe that intentional engagement in responsive practice demands both heart work and hard work, which are the key ingredients in a "perfect" recipe for becoming and being a good teacher. A good teacher not only is effective in teaching the subject matter (reflecting strong pedagogical knowledge and skills) but also cares about the children and their families by respecting their cultural and linguistic strengths and needs (reflecting positive professional dispositions). In sum, a good teacher engages in heart work that encompasses a profound sense of purpose and a steadfast commitment to teaching, coupled with a genuine care for children and their learning by understanding the developmental, cultural, linguistic, contextual factors surrounding them. It is driven by an inherent desire to make a positive impact on the lives of these children.

Heart work is a fundamental necessity, but not sufficient by itself. It must be accompanied by hard work. Hard work involves a resolute dedication to investing a significant amount of time, energy, and effort into enhancing both teaching and student learning by actively seeking out and participating in continuous professional development, such as acquiring cultural competence and learning to engage in responsive practice (as discussed in chapter 5). By investing in both heart work and hard work, educators can guide and inspire their students to do the same with their own learning as demonstrated in the case studies described and analyzed in this book (see chapters 6–8). Notably, in the case of educating learners from diverse backgrounds, particularly DLLs, teachers' conscious efforts to engage in practices that align with the Four Cornerstones of Responsive Practice framework represent not only a vital but also a sustainable means to put their heart work and hard work to work.

References

Ballantyne, Keira G., Alicia R. Sanderman, and Nicole McLaughlin. 2008. *Dual Language Learners in the Early Years: Getting Ready to Succeed in School*. Washington, DC: National Clearinghouse for English Language Acquisition. https://files.eric.ed.gov/fulltext/ED512635.pdf.

Bichay-Awadalla, Krystal, Cathy Huaqing Qi, Rebecca J. Bulotsky-Shearer, and Judith J. Carta. 2020. "Bidirectional Relationship between Language Skills and Behavior Problems in Preschool Children from Low-Income Families." *Journal of Emotional and Behavioral Disorders* 28 (2): 114–28. https://doi.org/10.1177/1063426619853535.

Borg, J. Rody, Mary O. Borg, and Harriet A. Stranahan. 2012. "Closing the Achievement Gap between High-Poverty Schools and Low-Poverty Schools." *Research in Business and Economics Journal* 5:1–24.

Brignell, Amanda, Katrina J. Williams, Sheena Reilly, and Angela T. Morgan. 2024. "Language Growth in Verbal Autistic Children from 5 to 11 Years." *Autism Research*, 1-10. https://doi.org/10.1002/aur.3171.

Brillante, Pamela, Jennifer J. Chen, Stephany Cuevas, Christyn Dundorf, Emily Brown Hoffman, Daniel R. Meier, Gayle Mindes, and Lisa R. Roy, eds. 2023. *Casebook: Developmentally Appropriate Practice in Early Childhood Programs Serving Children from Birth through Age 8*. Washington, DC: NAEYC.

Bronfenbrenner, Urie. 1979. *The Ecology of Human Development: Experiments by Nature and Design*. Cambridge, MA: Harvard University Press.

Chen, Jennifer J. 2014. "What Is Dual Language Immersion and What Does Research Say about Its Effectiveness?" In *Young Dual Language Learners: A Guide for PreK–3 Leaders*, edited by Karen N. Nemeth, 89–90. Philadelphia: Caslon.

———. 2015. "Effective Teaching Strategies for Facilitating the Language Acquisition of English Language Learners." *Idiom* 45 (2): 14–16.

———. 2016a. *Connecting Right from the Start: Fostering Effective Communication with Dual Language Learners*. Lewisville, NC: Gryphon House.

———. 2016b. "The Development of an Interlanguage: An Analysis of a Chinese Student's English Writing." *NYS TESOL Journal* 3 (1): 47–56.

———. 2019. "Cultural-Developmental Perspective: Chinese Immigrant Students' Academic Achievement Motivation as an Illustrative Example." *Online Readings in Psychology and Culture* 6 (1). https://doi.org/10.9707/2307-0919.1153.

———. 2022. "Pedagogical Adaptability as an Essential Capacity: Reflective Practice of Applying Theory to Practice among First Year Early Childhood Teachers during Remote Instruction." *Journal of Early Childhood Teacher Education* 44 (4): 723–46. https://doi.org/10.1080/10901027.2022.2147879.

———. 2023. "Reflecting on Reflection among Early Childhood Teachers: A Study of Reflection for, in, and on Action Intersecting with the Technical, Practical, and Critical Dimensions." *Reflective Practice* 24 (3): 324–46. https://doi.org/10.1080/14623943.2023.2194624.

Chen, Jennifer J., and Charlene B. Adams. 2022. "Drawing from and Expanding Their Toolboxes: Preschool Teachers' Traditional Strategies, Unconventional Opportunities, and Novel Challenges in Scaffolding Young Children's Social and Emotional Learning during Remote Instruction amidst COVID-19." *Early Childhood Education Journal* 51:925–37. https://doi.org/10.1007/s10643-022-01359-6.

Chen, Jennifer J., and Haily Badolato. 2023. "Scaffolding Social and Emotional Learning in Preschool Children from Low-Income Backgrounds: A Study of Teacher Strategies during COVID-19." *Education*, 3–13. https://doi.org/10.1080/03004279.2023.2168131.

Chen, Jennifer J., and Dana Battaglia. 2023. "Introduction and Book Overview." In *Casebook: Developmentally Appropriate Practice in Early Childhood Programs Serving Children from Birth through Age 8*, edited by Pamela Brillante, Jennifer J. Chen, Stephany Cuevas, et al., 1–5. Washington, DC: NAEYC.

Chen, Jennifer J., and Sonya de Groot Kim. 2014. "The Quality of Teachers' Interactive Conversations with Preschool Children from Low-Income Families during Small-Group and Large-Group Activities." *Early Years: An International Research Journal* 34 (3): 271–88. https://doi.org/10.1080/09575146.2014.912203.

Chen, Jennifer J., and Crystal Kacerek. 2022. "Leaders and Followers during Sociodramatic Play: A Study of Racial/Ethnic Minority Preschool Children from Socioeconomically Disadvantaged Backgrounds." *Journal of Research in Childhood Education* 36 (3): 517–40. https://doi.org/10.1080/02568543.2021.1960939.

Chen, Jennifer J., and Xiaoting Liang. 2017. "Teachers' Literal and Inferential Questions and Children's Responses: A Study of Teacher-Child Linguistic Interactions during Whole-Group Instruction in Hong Kong Kindergarten Classrooms." *Early Childhood Education Journal* 45 (5): 671–83. https://doi.org/10.1007/s10643-016-0807-9.

Chen, Jennifer J., and Yonggang Ren. 2019. "Relationships between Home-Related Factors and Bilingual Abilities among Chinese-English Dual Language Learners from Immigrant, Low-Income Backgrounds." *Early Childhood Education Journal* 47:381–93. https://doi.org/10.1007/s10643-019-00941-9.

References

Chen, Jennifer J., and Dahana E. Rivera-Vernazza. 2022. "Communicating Digitally: Building Preschool Teacher-Parent Partnerships via Digital Technologies during COVID-19." *Early Childhood Education Journal* 51:1189–1203. https://doi.org/10.1007/s10643-022-01366-7.

Chen, Jennifer J., and Suzanne H. Shire. 2011. "Strategic Teaching: Fostering Communication Skills in Diverse Young Learners." *Young Children* 66 (2): 20–27.

Cheung, Alan C., and Robert E. Slavin. 2012. "Effective Reading Programs for Spanish-Dominant English Language Learners (ELLs) in the Elementary Grades: A Synthesis of Research." *Review of Educational Research* 82 (4): 351–95. https://doi.org/10.3102/0034654312465472.

Collier, Virgina, and Wayne Thomas. 2017. "Validating the Power of Bilingual Schooling: Thirty-Two Years of Large-Scale, Longitudinal Research." *Annual Review of Applied Linguistics* 37:203–17. https://doi.org/10.1017/S0267190517000034.

Cummins, Jim. 1979. "Cognitive/Academic Language Proficiency, Linguistic Interdependence, the Optimum Age Question and Some Other Matters." *Working Papers on Bilingualism* 19:121–29.

———. 1980. "The Cross-Lingual Dimensions of Language Proficiency: Implications for Bilingual Education and the Optimal Age Issue." *TESOL Quarterly* 14 (2): 175–87. www.jstor.org/stable/3586312.

———. 1981. "The Role of Primary Language Development in Promoting Educational Success for Language Minority Students." In *Schooling and Language Minority Students: A Theoretical Framework*, edited by the California State Department of Education. Los Angeles: California State Department of Education.

———. 2000. *Language, Power and Pedagogy: Bilingual Children in the Crossfire.* Clevedon, UK: Multilingual Matters.

Darling-Lukemond, Linda, and Gary Sykes. 1999. *Teaching as the Learning Profession: Handbook of Policy and Practice.* San Francisco: Jossey-Bass.

Dewey, John. 1910. *How We Think.* Boston: D.C. Heath & Co.

———. 1933. *How We Think: A Restatement of the Relation of Reflective Thinking to the Educative Process.* Boston: D.C. Heath & Co.

Dietrich, Sandy, and Erik Hernandez. 2022. "Language Use in the United States: 2019." *American Community Survey Reports.* Washington, DC: US Census Bureau. www.census.gov/content/dam/Census/library/publications/2022/acs/acs-50.pdf.

Edwards, Carolyn, Lella Gandini, and George Forman, eds. 2012. *The Hundred Languages of Children: The Reggio Emilia Experience in Transformation.* 3rd ed. Westport, CT: Praeger.

Erdosi, Valeria, and Jennifer J. Chen. 2023. "Engaging Dual Language Learners in Conversation to Support Translanguaging during Small-Group Activities." In *Casebook: Developmentally Appropriate Practice in Early Childhood Programs Serving Children from Birth through Age 8*, edited by Pamela Brillante, Jennifer J. Chen, Stephany Cuevas, et al., 178–82. Washington, DC: NAEYC.

Fairchild, Henry Pratt. 1926. *The Melting-Pot Mistake*. Boston, MA: Little, Brown and Co.

Farver, Jo Ann M., Christopher J. Lonigan, and Steffanie Eppe. 2009. "Effective Early Literacy Skill Development for Young Spanish-Speaking English Language Learners: An Experimental Study of Two Methods." *Child Development* 80 (3): 703–19. https://doi.org/10.1111/j.1467-8624.2009.01292.x.

Fisher, Evelyn L. 2017. "A Systematic Review and Meta-Analysis of Predictors of Expressive-Language Outcomes among Late Talkers." *Journal of Speech, Language, and Hearing Research* 60 (10): 2935–48.

Fuller, Bruce. 2003. "Education Policy under Cultural Pluralism." *Educational Researcher* 32 (9): 15–24. https://www.jstor.org/stable/3700020.

Gleason, Philip. 1964. "The Melting Pot: Symbol of Fusion or Confusion?" *American Quarterly* 16 (1): 20–46.

Hammerness, Karen, Linda Darling-Hammond, John Bransford with David Berliner, Marilyn Cochran-Smith, Morva McDonald, and Kenneth Zeichner. 2005. "How Teachers Learn and Develop." In *Preparing Teachers for a Changing World: What Teachers Should Learn and Be Able to Do*, edited by Linda Darling-Lukemond and John Bransford, 358–89. San Francisco: Jossey-Bass.

Hazard, William R., and Madelon Stent. 1973. "Cultural Pluralism and Schooling: Some Preliminary Observations." In *Cultural Pluralism in Education: A Mandate for Change*. New York: Appleton-Century-Crofts.

Hirschman, Charles. 1983. "America's Melting Pot Reconsidered." *Annual Review of Sociology* 9 (1): 397–423.

Hollinger, David. 1995. *Postethnic America: Beyond Multiculturalism*. New York: Basic Books.

Individuals with Disabilities Education Act (IDEA) 2017. *Sec. 300.320 Definition of Individualized Education Program*. Washington, DC: US Department of Education. https://sites.ed.gov/idea/regs/b/d/300.320.

Irwin, Véronique, Ke Wang, Tabith Tezil, Jijun Zhang, Alison Filbey, Julie Jung, Farrah Bullock Mann, Rita Dilig, and Stephanie Parker. 2023. *Report on the Condition of Education 2023* (NCES 2023-144). Washington, DC: National Center for Education Statistics, US Department of Education. https://nces.ed.gov/pubsearch/pubsinfo.asp?pubid=2023144.

Kallen, Horace. 1915. "Democracy versus the Melting Pot." *Nation* 100 (2590): 190–94, 217–20.

Kennedy, John F. 1964. *A Nation of Immigrants*. New York: Harper & Row.

Kenty-Drane, Jessica L. 2009. "Early Isolation: Racial and Economic Segregation in US Public Elementary Schools." *Race, Gender & Class* 16 (2): 45–62. https://www.jstor.org/stable/41658860.

Krashen, Stephen D. 1985. *The Input Hypothesis: Issues and Implications*. London: Longman.

Leighton, Lindsay, and Mary Jane Harkins. 2010. "Teachers' Perceptions of Their Cultural Competencies: An Investigation into the Relationships among Teacher Characteristics and Cultural Competence." *Journal of Multicultural Education* 6 (2): 1–28.

Li, Hui, and Jennifer J. Chen. 2017. "Evolution of the Early Childhood Curriculum in China: The Impact of Social and Cultural Factors on Revolution and Innovation." *Early Child Development and Care* 187 (10): 1471–83. https://doi.org/10.1080/03004430.2016.1220373.

Migration Policy Institute. 2024. "U.S. Immigrant Population and Share over Time, 1850-Present." https://www.migrationpolicy.org/programs/data-hub/charts/immigrant-population-over-time.

Moll, Luis C., Cathy Amanti, Deborah Neff, and Norma Gonzalez. 1992. "Funds of Knowledge for Teaching: Using Qualitative Approach to Connect Homes and Classrooms." *Theory into Practice* 31 (2): 132–41.

NAEYC (National Association for the Education of Young Children). 2019. *NAEYC Early Learning Program Accreditation Standards and Assessment Items.* Washington, DC: NAEYC. www.naeyc.org/sites/default/files/globally-shared/downloads/PDFs/accreditation/early-learning/standards_assessment_2019.pdf.

———. 2020. "Developmentally Appropriate Practice." Position statement. Washington, DC: NAEYC. www.naeyc.org/sites/default/files/globally-shared/downloads/PDFs/resources/position-statements/dap-statement_0.pdf.

———. 2022. *Developmentally Appropriate Practice in Early Childhood Programs Serving Children from Birth through Age 8.* 4th ed. Washington, DC: NAEYC.

Office of Head Start. 2008. *Dual Language Learning: What Does It Take?* Washington, DC: US Department of Health and Human Services, Administration for Children and Families. https://eclkc.ohs.acf.hhs.gov/sites/default/files/pdf/dual-language-learning-what-does-it-take.pdf.

Office of Special Education Programs (OSEP). 2020. "OSEP Fast Facts: Children 3 through 5 Served under Part B, Section 619 of the IDEA." Washington, DC: US Department of Education. https://sites.ed.gov/idea/osep-fast-facts-children-3-5-20.

Osterman, Karen F., and Robert B. Kottkamp. 2004. *Reflective Practice for Educators.* 2nd ed. Thousand Oaks, CA: Corwin Press.

Park, Maki, Jie Zong, and Jeanne Batalova. 2018. *Growing Superdiversity among Young U.S. Dual Language Learners and Its Implications.* Washington, DC: Migration Policy Institute. www.migrationpolicy.org/sites/default/files/publications/SuperDiversityAmongDLLs_FINAL.pdf.

Phuntsog, Nawan. 2001. "Culturally Responsive Teaching: What Do Selected United States Elementary School Teachers Think?" *Intercultural Education* 12 (1): 51–64. https://doi.org/10.1080/14675980125627.

Piaget, Jean. 1963. *The Origins of Intelligence in Children.* New York: Norton.

Rezvan, Shahrzad Rezaee, Mahdieh Rezaee Rezvan, Seyedeh Nastaran Asad zadeh, Seyed Saeed Torabi, Moslem Taheri Soodejani, Hamed Ghasemzadehmoghaddam, Mehri Firozeh, Atefe sajedi, Faezeh Rohani & Nima Firouzeh, 2024. "The Efficacy of Cognitive -Behavioural Play Therapy and Puppet Play Therapy on Bilingual Children's Expressive, Receptive Language Disorders." *Early Child Development and Care* 194 (2): 296–307. https://doi.org/10.1080/03004430.2024.2309453.

Riojas-Cortez, Mari. 2001. "Preschoolers' Funds of Knowledge Displayed through Sociodramatic Play Episodes in a Bilingual Classroom." *Early Childhood Education Journal* 29:35–40. https://doi.org/10.1023/A:1011356822737.

Sandy, Jonathan, and Kevin Duncan. 2010. "Examining the Achievement Test Score Gap between Urban and Suburban Students." *Education Economics* 18 (3): 297–315. https://doi.org/10.1080/09645290903465713.

Schön, Donald A. 1983. *The Reflective Practitioner: How Professionals Think in Action*. New York: Basic Books.

———. 1987. *Educating the Reflective Practitioner: Toward a New Design for Teaching and Learning in the Professions*. San Francisco: Jossey-Bass.

Shonkoff, Jack P., and Deborah A. Phillips (Eds.). 2000. *From Neurons to Neighborhoods: The Science of Early Child Development*. National Academy Press.

Suh, Eunyoung Eunice. 2004. "The Model of Cultural Competence through an Evolutionary Concept Analysis." *Journal of Transcultural Nursing* 15 (2): 93–102. https://doi.org/10.1177/1043659603262488.

Tabors, Patton O., and Catherine E. Snow. 1994. "English as a Second Language in Preschools." In *Educating Second Language Children: The Whole Child, the Whole Curriculum, the Whole Community*, edited by Fred Genesee, 103–25. New York: Cambridge University Press.

Thomas, Wayne P., and Virginia P. Collier. 2002. *A National Study of School Effectiveness for Language Minority Students' Long-Term Academic Achievement*. Washington, DC: US Department of Education, Office of Educational Research and Improvement.

US Census Bureau. 2015. "Census Bureau Reports at Least 350 Languages Spoken in U.S. Homes." https://www.census.gov/newsroom/archives/2015-pr/cb15-185.html.

US Department of Education. 2024. "Protecting Students with Disabilities: Frequently Asked Questions about Section 504 and the Education of Children with Disabilities." Accessed February 19, 2024. www2.ed.gov/about/offices/list/ocr/504faq.html#:~:text=Section%20504%20requires%20that%20school,or%20more%20major%20life%20activities.

US Department of Health and Human Services and Administration for Children and Families. 2023. "Head Start Program Facts: Fiscal Year 2022." Accessed March 7, 2024. https://eclkc.ohs.acf.hhs.gov/data-ongoing-monitoring/article/head-start-program-facts-fiscal-year-2022.

Vaughn, Margaret. 2019. "Adaptive Teaching during Reading Instruction: A Multi-Case Study." *Reading Psychology* 40 (1): 1–33. https://doi.org/10.1080/02702711.2018.1481478.

Vertovec, Steven. 2007. "Super-Diversity and Its Implications." *Ethnic and Racial Studies* 30 (6): 1024–54. https://doi.org/10.1080/01419870701599465.

Vygotsky, Lev S. 1978. *Mind and Society: The Development of Higher Mental Processes*. Cambridge, MA: Harvard University Press.

Wasik, Barbara A., and Annemarie H. Hindman. 2015. "Talk Alone Won't Close the 30-Million Word Gap." *Phi Delta Kappan* 96 (6): 50–54. https://doi.org/10.1177/0031721715575300.

Weiland, Christina, and Hirokazu Yoshikawa. 2013. "Impacts of a Prekindergarten Program on Children's Mathematics, Language, Literacy, Executive Function, and Emotional Skills." *Child Development* 84 (6): 2112–30. https://doi.org/10.1111/cdev.12099.

West, Anne. 2007. "Poverty and Educational Achievement: Why Do Children from Low-Income Families Tend to Do Less Well at School?" *Benefits: A Journal of Poverty and Social Justice* 15 (3): 283–97. https://doi.org/10.51952/XLJA4165.

Wood, David, Jerome S. Brunner, and Gail Ross. 1976. "The Role of Tutoring in Problem Solving." *Journal of Child Psychology and Psychiatry* 17 (2): 89–100. https://doi.org/10.1111/j.1469-7610.1976.tb00381.x.

Index

academic success and CALP, 30–31, 64
adaptive expertise, described, 13–14
age appropriateness of learning experiences, 38
Ahmadein, Josephine, 72–75
American Community Survey (2011–2015), 19
American Community Survey (2019), 19
Arabic, 19, 21
assessments, 34, 87
assumptions, examining through reflective practices, 13

Bachelard, Gaston, 27
basic interpersonal communicative skills (BICS)
    acquisition of, 31
    defined, 30
    exposure and practice through social interactions for acquisition of, 63
    scaffolding receptive and expressive language skills in, 63
Battaglia, Dana, 35
behavior
    case studies
        family-teacher partnership, 75–82
        scaffolding preschooler's acquisition of language skills and engagement in effective, 51–55
    language skills and, 47
biases, examining through reflective practices, 13
bidirectional/two-way communication, 69
bilingual education, benefits for language development of, 33–34

bilingualism
    CUP and, 31
    language used by parents' and, of DLLs, 23
    superdiversity and traditional educational approach to, 25
    transfer of skills from one language to another, 25, 31–33
Bronfenbrenner, Urie, 67, 88

Carter, Jimmy, 17
Casebook: Developmentally Appropriate Practice in, Early Childhood Programs Serving Children from Birth through Age 8 (NAEYC), 35
Casella, Vanessa, 9, 104–106
case studies
    learners with special needs
        supporting communication needs of prekindergarteners, 100–103
        supporting learning of third graders, 104–106
        teaching preschoolers, 94–97
        teaching preschoolers and kindergarteners, 97–100
    scaffolding
        first graders and partnering with families and other teachers, 82–86
        kindergarteners' positive transfer of language skills, 55–58
        prekindergartener's acquisition of language skills and engagement in effective social interaction, 48–51

preschooler's acquisition of language skills using variety of strategies, 51–55
second grader's academic writing, 59–62
teacher-family partnership
family of infant, 72–75
family of preschooler, 75–82
first graders and partnering with other teachers and, 82–86
understanding IEP process, 78–82
Chinese
prevalence of households speaking, 19
as second most common home language of DDLs, 21
ClassDojo app, 69
cognitive academic language proficiency (CALP)
academic success and, 30–31, 64
acquisition of, 31
cognitive demands, 30–31
defined, 30
scaffolding receptive and expressive language skills in, 63
strategies for supporting development of, 64–66
time and explicit language instruction required for acquisition of, 63
Cohen, Dorothy H., 67
Collier, Virginia, 33
commonality
age appropriateness of learning experiences, 38
as core consideration of developmentally appropriate practice, 36
common underlying proficiency (CUP), 31–33
communication
case study of supporting, needs of prekindergarteners with special needs, 100–103
effective teacher-family, 69–71, 88
"seeking to understand and then be understood" approach to, 71
constructivism, 38

context
as core consideration of developmentally appropriate practice, 36
social, cultural, and linguistic, of children, 39
contextually responsive practices
case studies demonstrating examples of
acquisition of language skills by preschoolers and kindergarteners, 97–99, 100
partnership with families and other teachers of first graders, 82–84, 86
partnership with family of infant, 72–73, 74–75
partnership with family of preschooler, 75–77, 78
partnership with family of preschooler: understanding IEP process, 78–81, 82
scaffolding kindergarteners' positive transfer of language skills, 55–57, 58
scaffolding prekindergatener's acquisition of language skills and engagement in effective social interaction, 48–49, 51
scaffolding preschooler's acquisition of, using variety of strategies, 51–54, 55
scaffolding second grader's academic writing, 59–61, 62
supporting communication needs of prekindergarteners with special needs, 100–102, 103
supporting learning of third graders, 104–105, 106
teaching preschoolers with special needs, 94–95, 96–97
described, 41–42
countries of origin of DDLs and parents of, 21
creativity and technical rationality approach, 12
cultural competence, 40

culturally responsive practices
  case studies demonstrating examples of
    acquisition of language skills by preschoolers and kindergarteners, 97–100
    partnership with families of first grades, 82–84, 85
    partnership with family of infant, 72–73, 74
    partnership with family of preschooler, 75–78
    partnership with family of preschooler: understanding IEP process, 78–81
    partnership with other teachers of first graders, 82–84, 85
    scaffolding kindergarteners' positive transfer of language skills, 55–57
    scaffolding prekindergatener's acquisition of language skills and engagement in effective social interaction, 48–49, 50
    scaffolding preschooler's acquisition of, using variety of strategies, 51–54
    scaffolding second grader's academic writing, 59–61, 62
    supporting communication needs of prekindergarteners with special needs, 100–102, 103
    supporting learning of third graders, 104–105, 106teaching preschoolers with special needs, 94–95, 96
  described, 39–41
cultural mosaic model of United States, 18
cultural pluralism, 18
culture
  learning as activity embedded in, 45
  maintenance of home, 24–25
Cummins, Jim
  BICS and, 27, 30, 31
  CALP and, 27, 30, 31
  CUP and, 31

Dana, John Cotton, 109
decision making, using professional judgment and expertise, 4
developmentally appropriate practice
  areas under, 6
  commonality and, 38
  described, 35
  foundation of, 36
  reflecting on developmental, cultural, linguistic, and contextual characteristics of children in teaching, 42
developmentally responsive practices
  case studies demonstrating examples of
    acquisition of language skills by preschoolers and kindergarteners, 97–99
    partnership with families of first graders, 82–85
    partnership with family of infant, 72–74
    partnership with family of preschooler, 75–77
    partnership with family of preschooler: understanding IEP process, 78–81
    partnership with other teachers of first graders, 82–85
    scaffolding kindergarteners' positive transfer of language skills, 55–57
    scaffolding prekindergatener's acquisition of language skills and engagement in effective social interaction, 48–50
    scaffolding preschooler's acquisition of, using variety of strategies, 51–54
    scaffolding second grader's academic writing, 59–61
    supporting communication needs of prekindergarteners with special needs, 100–103
    supporting learning of third graders, 104–106

teaching preschoolers with special
  needs, 94–95
 described, 37–39
Dewey, John, 11
Diaz, Alexandra, 8, 75–78
Dietrich, Sandy, 19
digital tools, for communicating with
  families, 69–70
DiGuilio, Megan, 8, 48–51
disabilities, use of term, 92
diversity
 defining, 18
 Four Cornerstones of Responsive Practice framework and, 36
 of immigrants to United States, 18
 multiple approaches to teaching and, 39
 respect and understanding of cultural, 40–41
dual language immersion, benefits for language development of, 33–34
dual language learners (DLLs)
 defining, 3–4
 immigrants as, 20
 number of children, birth to eight, 20
 percent of preschool, served under IDEA, 93

early childhood education, defined, 9
early childhood educators. *See* teachers
education
 benefits for language development of bilingual, 33–34
 CALP and academic success, 30–31
 factors affecting quality of DLLs', 23–25
 level of parents of DDLs, 22
Enciso-Williams, Tiffany, 8–9, 94–97
English language, assessing expressive receptive language skills in home language and English, 29–30
equity
 Four Cornerstones of Responsive Practice framework and, 36
 multiple approaches to teaching and, 39
ethnicity of DLLs, 21
experience, reflecting on, 11

expressive language skills
 assessing, in home language and English, 29–30
 as complementary to receptive language skills, 28–29
 importance of, 34
 as mutually reinforcing to receptive language skills, 29
 scaffolding, 63

Fairchild, Henry Pratt, 17–18
families of dual language learners
 effective communication with, 69–71, 88
 effects of linguistic isolation of, 22
 family structure, 22
 income, 22
 parents as child's first teachers, 67
 parents in
  educational attainment, 22
  language used by, and bilingualism of DLLs, 23
  top countries of origin of, 21
 partnership with
  case study: family of infant, 72–75
  case study: family of preschooler, 75–78
  case study: family of preschooler, understanding IEP, 78–82
  case study: other teachers of first-graders and, 82–86
  establishing, 53–54
  factors influencing, 68–69
  importance of, 87–88, 110
  reasons for, 67–68
  reflecting on, 89
504 plans, 93
Four Cornerstones of Responsive Practice framework
 child as focal point of, 36
 contextual. *See* contextually responsive practices
 cornerstones of, 36–37
 cultural. *See* culturally responsive practices
 developmental. *See* developmentally responsive practices

importance of understanding DLLs and their families, 110
interconnection of, 7
linguistic. *See* linguistically responsive practices
practices advocated by, 36
reflecting on, 10
3CAPs framework and, 36

Gleason, Philip, 17–18
Google Translate
student use of, 61
using as part of linguistically responsive practice, 62
value of translations, 75, 76, 83
Groot Kim, Sonja de, 47
guidelines for professional practice, described, 36

Hernandez, Erik, 19
Hirschman, Charles, 17–18
Hmong, prevalence of households speaking, 19
Hollinger, David, 18
home language
assessing expressive language skills in, 29–30
assessing receptive language skills in, 29–30
case study of supporting infant's, 72–75
importance of promoting DLLs', 25
maintenance of
benefits of, 24–25
formal education in, and, 23
most common, 21
teacher's use of, 41, 48
How We Think: A Restatement of the Relation of Reflective Thinking to the Educative Process (Dewey), 11
hyperdiversity. *See* superdiversity

"iceberg" model, 32
immigrants
diversity of, to United States, 18
as dual language learners, 20
United States as nation of, 17–18

inclusion
Four Cornerstones of Responsive Practice framework and, 36
multiple approaches to teaching and, 39
teaching in prekindergarten, classroom, 78–82
inclusive approach to communication, 71
inclusivity
Four Cornerstones of Responsive Practice framework and, 36
multiple approaches to teaching and, 39
income of families of DLLs, 22
individuality, as core consideration of developmentally appropriate practice, 36, 39
individualized education programs (IEPs)
case studies
acquisition of language skills by preschoolers and kindergarteners, 97–100
supporting communication needs of prekindergarteners, 100–103
supporting learning of third graders with special needs, 104–106
case studies of, partnership with family to understand, 78–82
described, 93
Individuals with Disabilities Education Act (IDEA), 92–93
intentionality, applying in planning and delivering learning experiences, 5–6
"interdependence hypothesis," 31–32
Irwin, Véronique, 91–92

Kacerek, Crystal, 39
Kallen, Horace, 18
Kaufman, Samantha, 8, 78–82
Kennedy, John F., 17
Krashen, Stephen D., 63

language disorders or delays, receptive and expressive abilities in children with, 30
language(s)
acquisition of

developmental sequence of, 29
scaffolding of, 47
second, 64
effects of linguistic isolation of families of DLLs, 22
importance of, 3
inherent beauty in, 27
most common spoke in homes of DDLs, 21
sharing proficiencies among, 31–33
superdiversity of spoken, in United States, 19–20
See also bilingualism; home language
language skills
ability to transfer communicative and cognitive, from one language to another, 25, 31–33
BICS and effective communication, 30
CALP and effective communication, 30
case studies
acquisition of, in self-contained special education classroom of preschoolers and kindergartners, 97–100
kindergarteners' positive transfer of, 55–58
scaffolding prekindergartener's acquisition of, and engagement in effective social interaction, 48–51
scaffolding preschooler's acquisition of, using variety of strategies, 51–55
receptive, and expressive, needed, 28–30
reflecting on scaffolding, 34, 66
social interactions and, 46–47
transfer of, from one language to another, 25, 31–33
See also cognitive academic language proficiency (CALP)
leadership and language skills, 47
learners with special needs
case studies
prekindergarteners in self-contained classroom, 100–103
supporting learning of third graders, 104–106
teaching preschoolers and kindergarteners with, 97–100
teaching preschoolers with, 94–97
reflecting on working with, 108
statistics about, 92–93
strategies to support, 107
learning
as culturally embedded activity, 45
experiences
age appropriateness of, 38
applying intentionality in planning and delivering, 5–6
individual experience as key to, 38
through social interaction as critical to development, 38
Li, Hui, 36
linguistically responsive practices
case studies demonstrating examples of
acquisition of language skills by preschoolers and kindergarteners, 97–99, 100
partnership with families and teachers of first graders, 82–84, 85–86
partnership with family of infant, 72–73, 74
partnership with family of preschooler, 75–77, 78
partnership with family of preschooler: understanding IEP process, 78–81, 82
scaffolding kindergarteners' positive transfer of language skills, 55–57, 58
scaffolding prekindergatener's acquisition of language skills and engagement in effective social interaction, 48–49, 50–51
scaffolding preschooler's acquisition of, using variety of strategies, 51–55
supporting communication needs of prekindergarteners with special needs, 100–102, 103
supporting learning of third graders, 104–105, 106

teaching preschoolers with special needs, 94–95, 96
described, 41
listening comprehension, as receptive language skill, 28
literacy, CALP and, 30–31

The Melting Pot (Zangwill), 17
melting pot model of United States, 17–18
Migration Policy Institute, 17
multilingualism and ability to transfer communicative and cognitive skills from one language to another, 25, 31–33

National Association for the Education of Young Children (NAEYC)
  applying intentionality in planning and delivering learning experiences, 5–6
  areas under developmentally appropriate practice, 6
  Casebook: Developmentally Appropriate Practice in Early Childhood Programs Serving Children from Birth through Age 8, 35
  definition of early childhood education, 9
  developmentally responsive practice, 37–39
  importance of incorporating knowledge of diverse contexts within which each child develops and learns, 41
  teacher's reciprocal partnerships with families, 68

Papoutsakis, Helen, 8, 82–86
parents. *See* families of dual language learners
Park, Maki, 19, 20, 21–22
pedagogical adaptability
  components of, 14
  defined, 14
  developing and integrating reflective action in teaching, 14–15

Perez, ChareMone', 8, 59–62
Piaget, Jean, 38
preconceived notions, examining through reflective practices, 13
"pre-production" stage of learning second language, 63–64
problem solving, 12
professional development
  cultural competence and, 40, 87
  linguistic competence and, 87

race of DLLs, 21
Rafhan, Fatima, 8, 51–55
reading comprehension, as receptive language skill, 28
receptive language skills
  assessing, in home language and English, 29–30
  as complementary to expressive language skills, 28–29
  importance of, 34
  as mutually reinforcing to expressive language skills, 29
  scaffolding, 63
reflection-for-action, 13
reflection-in-action, 13
reflection-on-action, 13, 15
reflective practices
  benefits of, 15–16
  contextual factors considered, 5
  cultural competence and, 40
  described, 11
  developing and integrating, in teaching, 14–15
  examining assumptions, biases, and preconceived notions, 13
  identifying areas of strength and weakness, 12–13
  importance of, 4, 111
  intentionality in, 5–6
  learning from experience and, 11
  for open-ended, nontechnical problems, 12
  power of, 5–6
  as promoting continuous learning cycle, 13
  questions for, 16

Four Cornerstones of Responsive
    Practice framework, 10
  learners with special needs, 108
  scaffolding acquisition of different
    language skills, 34
  scaffolding strategies for social
    interaction and language
    development, 66
  for superdiversity, 26
  teacher-family partnerships, 89
  ways of incorporating develop-
    mental, cultural, linguistic, and
    contextual characteristics of
    children in teaching, 42
  stages of, 13
Reggio Emilia approach, 39
Report on the Condition of Education 2023
  (Irwin), 91–92
rhyming, 55–58
Riojas-Cortez, Mari, 39
Rivera-Vernazza, Dahana, 70
Rogers, Fred, 91
Ruiz, Lissette Y., 9, 100–103

salad bowl model of United States, 18
"sandwich" approach to communication,
  70–71
scaffolding
  acquisition of second language, 64, 65
  assessments and, 34
  case studies
    first graders and partnering with
      families and other teachers,
      82–86
    kindergarteners' positive transfer of
      language skills, 55–58
    prekindergartener's acquisition of
      language skills and engagement
      in effective social interaction,
      48–51
    preschooler's acquisition of lan-
      guage skills using variety of
      strategies, 51–55
    second grader's academic writing,
      59–62
  described, 46
  language acquisition, 47

  receptive and expressive language
    skills, 63
  reflecting on
    acquisition of language skills, 34
    strategies for social interaction and
      language development, 66
    zone of proximal development and, 45
Schön, Donald, 11–12
"seeking to understand and then
  be understood" approach to
  communication, 71
self-reflection and cultural competence,
  40
Shire, Suzanne, 107
"silent period" of learning second
  language, 63–64
Snow, Catherine E., 64
social interactions
  case studies
    scaffolding prekindergartener's
      acquisition of language skills and
      engagement in effective, 48–51
    scaffolding preschooler's acqui-
      sition of language skills and
      engagement in effective, 51–55
  language skills and, 46–47
  as necessary for acquisition of BICS, 63
  reflecting on scaffolding strategies for,
    66
social justice
  Four Cornerstones of Responsive Prac-
    tice framework and, 36
  multiple approaches to teaching and,
    39
social learning, importance of, 45
socioecological theory, 67, 88
Spanish, 19, 21
special education. *See* learners with
  special needs
Stiles, Imelda, 8, 55–58
"Strategic Teaching: Fostering Communication Skills in Diverse Young Learner"
  (Chen and Shire), 107
superdiversity
  described, 18
  factors contributing to, 21
  reflecting on, 26

of spoken languages in United States, 19–20
traditional educational approach to bilingualism and, 25

Tabors, Patton O., 64
Tagalog, 21
teachers
   case studies of
      partnerships with, and families for first-graders, 82–86
      partnerships with other educators for preschooler, 75–78
   continual learning by, 109, 110
   cultural competence of, 40
   effective communication with families, 69–71, 88
   importance of partnerships with other educators, 88
   importance of reflection by, 4, 111
   parents as child's first, 67
   pedagogical adaptability of, 14
   pedagogic effectiveness of, 4
   support system for, 86–88, 110
   unique perspectives of, 5
   use of child's home language by, 41
   use of technical rationality approach by, 12
   See also partnership with *under* families of dual language learners

technical rationality approach, 11–12
Thomas, Wayne, 33
3CAPs framework, Four Cornerstones of Responsive Practice framework and, 36
three core considerations, 36
Tools of the Mind curriculum, 100
total physical response (TPR) technique, 52–53

unidirectional/one-way communication, 69
United States
   diversity of immigrants to, 18
   as nation of immigrants, 17–18
   superdiversity of spoken languages in, 19–20

Vaccaro, Erin, 9, 97–100
Vaughn, Margaret, 14
Vertovec, Steven, 18
Vietnamese, 21
Vygotsky, Lev, 38, 45

Wood, David, 46
writing, case study of scaffolding second grader's academic, 59–62

Zangwill, Israel, 17
zone of proximal development (ZPD), 45–46

About the Author

Jennifer J. Chen, EdD, is full professor and chair of the Department of Early Childhood Education at Kean University in New Jersey. Prof. Chen earned her Doctor of Education in human development and psychology from Harvard Graduate School of Education, her Master of Education in language and literacy also from Harvard, her Master of Arts in bilingual and bicultural education from Teachers College, Columbia University, and her Bachelor of Arts in psychology (with a minor in linguistics) from Barnard College, Columbia University. She is a well-respected leader in the field of early childhood education and early childhood teacher education through her professional and scholarly contributions. Notably, she served as the former president of the New Jersey Association of Early Childhood Teacher Educators (NJAECTE), former copresident of the NJAECTE, and former chair of the inaugural research committee for the National Association of Early Childhood Teacher Educators (NAECTE).

Prof. Chen is also an award-winning researcher, distinguished scholar, distinguished college teacher, and research mentor. The numerous honors that have been bestowed on Prof. Chen include the 2023 NAECTE Foundation's Outstanding Early Childhood Teacher Educator Award, a 2023 Exchange Leader in the Exchange Leadership Initiative in the field of Early Care and Education, the 2022 NJAECTE's Distinguished Scholarship in Early Childhood Teacher Education/Early Childhood Education Award, the 2021 Kean Presidential Excellence Award for Distinguished Scholarship, the 2020 NAECTE Foundation's Established Career Award for Research on Early Childhood Teacher Education, the Kean Presidential Excellence Award for Distinguished Teaching, the Kean Faculty Research Mentor of the Year award, a Fulbright Scholar research award to Hong Kong, a book winner award, and many university research awards.

As of 2024, Prof. Chen has contributed more than ninety authored/coauthored scholarly publications in the fields of psychology and education (especially early childhood education and early childhood teacher education), including three books (not counting this one), coedited volumes, and many refereed research articles in reputable academic journals. Her previous book contribution about dual language learners, *Connecting Right from the Start: Fostering Effective Communication with Dual Language Learners*, was published by Gryphon House in 2016.